About the Author

Writer and journalist David Long has regularly appeared in *The Times* and the *London Evening Standard*, as well as on TV and radio. He has written a number of books on London, including *Spectacular Vernacular, Tunnels Towers & Temples* and the highly successful *Little Book of London*. He lives in Suffolk, England. Find him online at www.davidlong.info.

A HISTORY
of LONDON *in*
100 PLACES

DAVID LONG

ONEWORLD

A Oneworld Book

First published in North America, Great Britain & Austalia by
Oneworld Publications 2014

ISBN 978-1-78074-413-1
ISBN 978-1-78074-414-8 (eBook)

Text designed and typeset by Tetragon Publishing
Printed and bound by CPI Group (UK) Ltd, Croydon, CR0 4YY

Oneworld Publications
10 Bloomsbury Street
London WC1B 3SR
England

CONTENTS

INTRODUCTION

A great world city shaped by invasion, occupation and immigration, by upheavals as diverse as the Great Fire, the Blitz and the Big Bang, London may no longer be the largest metropolis – it lost the lead to New York a hundred years ago – but after two thousand years its history and its cultural heritage are unmatched.

Walk the streets today and it is hard to ignore what went before. The city may reinvent itself on an almost perpetual basis, the skyline always pricked by cranes and skeletons of steel, but everywhere there are clues to London's past.

Besides Roman walls, Saxon fish traps and Norman churches, there are medieval markets that are still trading today, surviving fragments of great monastic foundations, timber-framed houses that against all odds managed to withstand the flames of 1666, and elegant streets and squares from the earliest exercises in practical town planning. Best of all, the vast majority of them can be visited, often at no charge, and on such visits readers will find this book to be a useful companion.

It is true that very little is known of the time before the Romans arrived, that their first settlement was more or less destroyed by Boudicca and her Iceni warriors, and that many later iterations of London lie buried deep beneath huge new developments in and around the Square Mile.* But across the capital fresh discoveries are still being made all the time and, while much of the past remains elusive, Londoners and visitors to their city are genuinely spoilt for choice when setting out to explore its long riotous history.

Some of the most evocative relics of past centuries are still to be found complete in all their splendour, classed as world-famous buildings; others are just foundations or the outline of a place – or even, in the case of the great frost fairs, no more than contemporary accounts of what went on upon the frozen Thames. But from these remains emerges a picture of London that is as vibrant, as unique and as incredible as anything we see around the city today. Fast moving, always changing, and never standing still: it is a place we can relate to – and that we can literally reach out and touch.

---

* The term Square Mile has long been used to describe the old walled capital – what we now know as the City of London – although following boundary changes in the 1990s, which incorporated a small area to the north, its true extent is now an irritatingly precise 1.16 square miles.

Chapter 1

ROMAN LONDINIUM

There is frustratingly little to know of London before the coming of the Roman legions. Beyond a few random pottery shards and an Iron Age burial within what are now the precincts of the Tower of London, there is no conclusive evidence for any real settlement ahead of Julius Caesar's arrival in 54 BC. The likelihood is that people were already scratching out a living of sorts somewhere along the wide, marshy valley of the Thames – traces of a Bronze Age footpath have been found in Plumstead – but no one can say with certainty where they might have lived, or how.

For the Romans, however, the river provided an obvious line of defence. In AD 43 soldiers of the second invasion force (in the reign of Claudius) ran a bridge from one side to the other, and it is around this that Londinium can be said to have developed. Both bridge* and settlement were famously destroyed by Boudicca and an avenging Iceni army in AD 60. A thick layer of ash attests to this, more than ten feet below today's street level – and writing only a few years later the Roman historian Tacitus confirms that at the time of its destruction the settlement had been thriving, a place 'filled with traders and a celebrated centre of commerce'.

1. London Wall

Tower Hill, City of London, EC3

Militarily the early trading post had been of little importance, but following the carnage of Boudicca's ferocious onslaught – Tacitus tells of literally thousands being 'massacred, hanged, burned and crucified' – a fortress was built in the north-western part of the city that we call Cripplegate. Later, in the third century, a defensive wall was thrown up around the remainder.

---

* This may have been a floating pontoon-type initially, although a more conventional fixed bridge followed in due course. Remarkably, this second structure was to provide the supports for several Saxon and medieval replacements, the original Roman piers continuing to underpin each new crossing until Sir John Rennie's 'New London Bridge' of 1831.

The finished wall – in parts eight feet thick and as much as fifteen feet high – enclosed an area of 330 acres, making London by far the largest city in Britain and the fifth largest in the part of the Roman Empire that lay to the north of the Alps. It was built largely of Kentish ragstone on foundations of flint and compacted clay, a hard grey limestone – a rarity in south-east England – that was to prove ideal for building strong and durable structures of this sort.

As well as some twenty-one bastions the wall incorporated six gateways – Aldgate, Aldersgate, Bishopsgate, Cripplegate, Ludgate and Newgate – that led out to the great Roman roads linking the city to the rest of England. In civil engineering terms, the whole structure was a major undertaking even by Roman standards, requiring an estimated thirteen thousand barge loads of stone to

be brought up the River Medway and along the Thames from quarries located close to modern Maidstone.

Repaired, restored and where necessary improved, it was to enclose the city for more than one thousand five hundred years and the gates were only finally taken down in the mid-eighteenth century when they began to impede the traffic. Much of the stonework disappeared in the decades that followed their removal, but the surviving portions were nevertheless substantial enough that, following the Blitz, they were still among the tallest structures within that part of historic central London that today we know as the Square Mile.

Today various bits of the wall lie hidden in basements and cellars (for example, in the Old Bailey) but the most impressive fragments are those around the Barbican, on Noble Street and Cooper's Row, and on Tower Hill. The upper courses are mostly medieval (at one point crenellations were added, although these have gone), but with their distinctive lines of red brick or tile bonding the Roman work is easy to identify. Still rising to a height of more than twelve feet, it represents perhaps the most evocative reminder of London's earliest times.

2. First-century Wharf

Lower Thames Street, City of London, EC3

A fascinating riverside church that deserves more regard than it gets, St Magnus the Martyr is primarily known for one thing – and that is the portion of medieval London Bridge that is housed in its porch. Charles Dickens called the church one of the 'giant warders of the ancient bridge' as it stood at the northern end, its southern counterpart being the church of St Saviour and St Mary Overie, which in 1905 was reborn as Southwark Cathedral (see chapter 4).

Far smaller than the surviving portion of the old bridge, however, but arguably even more precious, is a chunk of wood that was brought to the church after being dug up by workmen who found it nearby in the 1930s. Mounted on a low stand in the porch, the chunk of wood is clearly labelled – FROM ROMAN WHARF. AD 75: FOUND FISH STREET HILL 1931 – but is nevertheless often missed by visitors coming to view Sir Christopher Wren's interior.

The existence of such wharfs had long been known about and in the 1970s the Museum of London conducted a detailed search along this stretch of the river. Among the discoveries were a second-century river wall, a third-century quayside described as being of 'ambitious' design, and numerous small finds of the sort that prove vital when it comes to extending our knowledge of domestic and commercial life in Roman London.

Beneath the pavement on the southern side of the street were found traces of a timber embankment wall, evidence of an early land reclamation scheme that would have helped push Roman London out beyond the line of the old wharf mentioned on the St Magnus plaque. Once again, from an engineering standpoint the work is highly impressive, with several tiers of large oak beams supported by piles and bracing, and there is evidence of many tons of earth and rubble being used as infill.

For all the strength and sophistication, however, the same evidence points to the new wharf being very short-lived. In fact, with nothing to suggest it was still in use after AD 260, its working life may have been as little as twenty years. The reasons for this are not fully understood, but the river level may have dropped causing channels to silt up, and certainly Saxon pirates are known to have been disrupting shipping routes to the continent by this time. Political and economic changes within the Roman Empire were also beginning to affect London's trading partners in northern Europe, and within a decade of the wharf's completion such an extensive construction may have been considered surplus to requirements. Certainly nothing else on this scale was to be constructed here for at least the next eight hundred years.

3. Roman Barge

Blackfriars, City of London, EC4

During the construction in 1962 of a vehicle underpass close to the meeting point of the Fleet River and the Thames, the remains were uncovered of a fifty-two-foot sailing barge, flat-bottomed and with a full load of the aforementioned Kentish limestone. Coins and pottery found with the wreck pointed to a mid-second-century date, something confirmed by later dendrochronological testing to establish the precise age of the wood used to construct the vessel. This suggests that the cargo formed part of the huge consignment ordered by city administrators for the construction of their new defensive wall.

In the waterlogged remains researchers quickly identified the bottom and parts of the collapsed port side of a traditional Romano-Celtic ship, a carvel-built vessel of oak with two broad keel-planks in place of a conventional keel. Between stempost and sternpost, the planks were fastened by large iron nails to oak frames with substantial floor timbers in the bottom and much lighter side frames above. The mast step, a rectangular socket about one-third of the length along from the bow, was located in a hefty transverse floor timber.

The find was hugely significant, but the surviving portion was too fragile and fragmentary to give a lay person a real impression of the builder's expertise and, indeed, the true scale of the vessels plying the Thames at this time. For this reason, and doubtless to gain a better understanding of Roman shipbuilding methods, the Museum of London subsequently authorized its ancient woodwork specialist Damian Goodburn to create a full-size replica.

This exciting project was based on measurements taken during the original excavation, and from plans drawn up from these. Using the latter, Goodburn was able to calculate the number and size of planks required, many of which were sourced from Kent where a large number of oaks had been felled in the Great Storm of 1987. Others came from trees that had grown into the appropriate shape, naturally curved timbers of this sort being generally far stronger than curved planks cut from a straight bough.

By using traditional tools – such as a two-man saw, adzes and hand axes – the finished replica stayed remarkably close to the original vessel, even including similar distinctive diagonal markings on the planks to those seen on other pieces of Roman-era timber found in and around the City. The work was carried out in the open, in full view of the public in the museum's small garden, before the barge was put on temporary display in 1991 together with a conserved section of Roman quayside.

4. Temple of Mithras

Queen Victoria Street, City of London, EC4

Originally located on the bank of the Walbrook (one of London's many 'lost rivers', several of which are now little more than sewers), the Mithraeum was discovered in the summer of 1954, a pagan temple the remains of which clearly indicated the outline of the walls, a triple apse and paired rows of supporting pillars.

Initially it was hoped that the structure would turn out to be an early Christian site, but with the ruins were found representations of a number of Roman gods, including Mercury, Venus and Minerva. The discovery of a marble bust of Mithras a few weeks later provided the final proof that the site was pagan, as did an early fourth-century inscription: PRO SALVTE D N CCCC ET NOB CAES DEO MITHRAE ET SOLI INVICTO AB ORIENTE AD OCCIDENTEM ('For the Salvation of our Lords the four Emperors and the noble Caesar, and to the god Mithras, the Invincible Sun from the east to the west').

The cult of Mithras – an austere religious movement that placed special emphasis on strength, courage and direct action – is known to have been particularly favoured by soldiers. Its iconography included bloodthirsty representations  of Mithras slaying a wild bull, a popular image used to symbolize man's journey from cradle to grave. A carved relief showing just such an epic struggle had been pulled from the Walbrook several decades earlier,* and was dedicated to Ulpius Silvanus, a veteran of a 2nd Legion of Augustus. It is thus to be assumed that he must have taken part in ceremonies performed in this very temple, the interior kept dark and mysterious to remind new initiates that it was in a cave that Mithras slew the sacred bull from whose blood all life flowed.

Interest in the find was enormous at the time. When the site was opened to the public more than one hundred thousand visitors queued to see it within the first five days, and there were calls in Parliament for it to be preserved *in situ.* The endless development and redevelopment that

---

*   This location has continued to throw up treasures, with more than ten thousand artefacts having been unearthed here at the time of writing, and excited media chatter about the discovery of a new 'Pompeii of the North'.

characterizes city life meant that this was not possible, however, and the decision was taken to dismantle the temple carefully so that its stones could be reassembled a couple of hundred yards from its original position.

In the event, the remains went into storage for nearly eight years, but thereafter and for the next fifty years the temple was visible to anyone walking along Queen Victoria Street. At the time of writing, the area is being redeveloped once again, and consideration is being given to returning the Mithraeum to its original site on the banks of the vanished river.

5. Amphitheatre

Guildhall Art Gallery, City of London, EC2

The Temple of Mithras remains the only Roman building in London in which one can see the entire plan laid out on the ground, but in 1987 a far more extensive structure was uncovered in the area bounded by Aldermanbury, Gresham Street and Basinghall Street.

The discovery was of a Roman amphitheatre, a large oval more than three hundred feet at its widest extent and centred on what is now Guildhall Yard. Originally it would have been of timber, and has been dated from the period of reconstruction following Boudicca's assault. But in the early second century it was rebuilt more substantially in stone, making it the largest in Britannia with a capacity of six thousand to seven thousand spectators (or around a quarter of London's population). In this form it remained in use until the departure of the Romans in the early fifth century.

Interestingly, the presence of such an important building continued to exercise a marked influence on the development of this area long after that date. For example, the likelihood is that the original Saxon Guildhall – a place for 'folkmoots', the general assembly of the townspeople – was deliberately located on the same site, and today the above-named streets still respect the original oval boundary rather than cutting across it.

Such a massive site could not, even so, have been left undeveloped for long once the Romans had left; nor following the discovery of the amphitheatre was its removal and relocation a viable option as it had been for the much smaller Mithraeum. Instead, imaginative steps have been taken to preserve something meaningful, and today the outline of the actual arena is clearly marked out in the paving of Guildhall Yard, and in the basement of the Guildhall Art Gallery partial remains of the main entrance are available to view. Visitors here can also see two small vestibules, possibly where combatants would have gathered before each performance, and part of a drainage system in which were found animal and human remains – presumably from those who took part in the famously grisly performances.

6. Mosaic Pavement

All Hallows by the Tower, City of London, EC3

Coloured mosaics and tessellated floors and pavements are among the most exciting relics from this era, and the discovery of this large section of mosaic – with its limestone-bordered red, yellow, black and white tesserae – in the City of London in 1976 is still considered to be one of the decade's biggest finds. Sealed for centuries beneath a layer of thick grey silt – on a site in Milk Street, between Cheapside and Gresham Street – the mosaic was carefully lifted and eventually put on display at the Museum of London.

Other, equally striking examples can be seen in the small museum at the Bank of England and at the British Museum, but beneath the church of All Hallows by the Tower it is thrillingly still possible to see a section of Roman pavement in its original position.

With a foundation date of 675 the church is conceivably London's oldest, as we shall see in the next chapter. The site was clearly occupied long before this date, however, and in 1926, during work in the crypt, a wonderful fragment of second-century red mosaic was uncovered beneath the foundations of the east wall. Perfectly preserved in the ancient undercroft, it is thought to have formed part of the floor of a domestic dwelling that stood here centuries before the church's endowment by a seventh-century Bishop of London. The same crypt is also home to a modern scale-model of Londinium, providing visitors with a bird's-eye view of the city seen from a vantage point across the Thames and somewhere in the area where the Shard now stands.

7. London's Last Roman Citizen

St Martin-in-the-Fields, Trafalgar Square, WC2

As recently as 2006 the BBC reported the historically significant discovery of a skeleton during building works at this landmark London church. The body was found in a Roman limestone coffin, secreted between some Victorian vaults and the boundary of the property, and was missing its head.

Not for the first time with burials, the find was initially wrongly dated and, like a similar discovery when the church was being built in the eighteenth century, the body was assumed to be a more recent interment reusing an old sarcophagus. In order to verify this a small portion of bone was sent for carbon dating, but to the delight of researchers, historians and the church authorities the results showed with considerable certainty that the person had died between AD 390 and AD 420.

The date is critical, AD 410 being the year that the Romans finally withdrew to the continent. Having recognized they could no longer defend their hard-pressed empire at its greatest extent, the legions were prepared to sacrifice or at least abandon outposts such as Britannia. The same date also means that 'London's last Roman' was a near-contemporary of St Martin himself – a Roman soldier born in Pannonia, a large region west of the Danube incorporating parts of Austria, Hungary and the territory of the former Yugoslavia – and suggests that the site has been of religious importance for far longer than had hitherto been supposed.

Intriguingly the same excavations also revealed the fragmentary remains of a simple, grey Saxon pot, one of the earliest of its type ever found. Lying just a few feet away from the coffin, and thought to be more than fifteen hundred years old, the discovery provided an important missing link between Roman Londinium and Anglo-Saxon Lundenwic – a much smaller settlement that is now known to have been centred not on the old walled city but beneath the modern West End.

Chapter 2

SAXON LUNDENWIC

With regard to London the long centuries we know as the Dark Ages seem especially well named. Our knowledge of Roman Londinium may even now be patchy and tantalizingly incomplete, but the archaeological record for the period is astonishingly rich and varied when viewed alongside the paucity of Anglo-Saxon finds.

There is, for example, nothing to be seen of the first cathedral dedicated to St Paul, although we know absolutely that it was founded by London's first bishop, Mellitus, in AD 604. Instead, for a long time the fate of the Roman city could only be guessed at, and expert opinion remained divided as to whether Saxon invaders ignored it, sacked it, or casually occupied its ruins as some kind of post-Roman slumland.

8. Saxon Arch

All Hallows by the Tower, City of London, EC3

The idea of post-Roman London as no more than small scattered communities – rough, ignorant squatters eking out a poor living in the ruins of a culture they could never understand – is bleak but strangely engaging. It is also quite reasonable: the Saxons were after all soldiers and farmers not townspeople, and as tribal folk they were more used to living in hamlets than in anything one might describe as an urban environment.

The lack of any compelling archaeological evidence to support the theory is regrettable, but it could be due to the nature of Saxon building methods, which relied mostly on wood, a material that can leave only the faintest traces in the ground (assuming these are not entirely obliterated by subsequent development).

Happily there are a few exceptions, and one such can be seen by visitors to the aforementioned church of All Hallows by the Tower. As long ago as 675, many miles to the east, another Bishop of London, Eorconweald, had founded a new abbey at Barking in Essex. To fund its development he presented the new abbey with several potentially valuable endowments, one of them being the land on which the first church was built on what is now Byward Street.

Despite appearances the present building is an extensive reconstruction following the near-total destruction during the Blitz of this rare survivor of the Great Fire of London. The walls are nevertheless substantially of the fifteenth century, but elsewhere in the building it is possible to discern components of various earlier incarnations. These include a simple but well-proportioned Saxon arch, which by great good fortune was rediscovered following widespread destruction in this area by wartime bombing.

More recently the archway has been identified as the oldest example of church architecture anywhere in the capital, solid evidence of a simple but quite substantial building and also the sole surviving example in London of an above-ground Saxon structure. The material used in its construction is also noteworthy, the Saxons' gradual transition from wooden buildings to stone ones being here achieved by scavenging and reusing Roman bricks and tiles of the sort already described in the section on the old City walls.

If not exactly widespread the practice of salvaging materials in this way was far from unique, and beneath Cheapside the crypt of St Mary-le-Bow also incorporates recycled pieces of Roman work. Saxon foundations have been identified in a number of other London churches too – including the famous St Bride's on Fleet Street, the seventh church on this one site – but nowhere else in the capital is there anything to rival All Hallows, or as easy for the visitor to explore and understand.

9. Fish Trap

Nine Elms, Lambeth, SW8

Visible only at low tide, and then hardly at all, a series of sodden wooden posts, two lines of them sunk deep into the muddy foreshore, is more typical of Saxon sites in London. Situated well away from the settlement's centre, and easily missed, the posts are all that remain of an Anglo-Saxon fish trap. Such devices were constructed to prevent fish retreating with the water when the tide turned, this particular one lying close to Vauxhall Bridge at the junction of the Thames and the River Effra.

Today it is easy to overlook the opaque brown Thames as a viable source of food, but at the time these posts were driven into the riverbed (sometime between AD 550 and AD 670) it would have been a rich and important resource for those living along its banks. The remains of several similar traps have been found at Kew, Barn Elms and Hammersmith – the latter an even older one, early fifth century – together with a *scramasax* or *seax*, the short-bladed weapon from which the Saxons derived their name.

A later version has also been found at Chelsea. Dated to some time between 730 and 900 this is slightly better preserved, but all of them exhibit a similar form, which is an ingenious v-shape with a long 'neck' in which the trapped fish can be held. The posts are typically no more than three or four inches in diameter, all roughly worked, and the sides would almost certainly have been hurdles of willow or wattle, although nothing of these survives.

The idea was simple, and the work must have been cold, uncomfortable and potentially highly dangerous. But the operation was also a relatively sophisticated one and, depending on the orientation of the trap, the builders of the traps could expect to harvest either salmon swimming upstream or (as at Chelsea) eels coming down. The traps were extremely efficient too, and continued to be used for centuries, our own word 'weir' coming from the Saxon *wer*, meaning a device to trap fish.

10. Grim's Dyke

Harrow Weald, HA3

A large country house of the 1870s designed by Richard Norman Shaw, the Grim's Dyke Hotel was once home to W.S. Gilbert of comic opera fame and the scene of his accidental death by drowning. To modern ears, the place sounds more Yorkshire than London, but the hotel takes its name from this ancient earthwork that stretches nearly three miles from Harrow Weald to Pinner Green.

Known variously as Grim's Dyke, Grime's Dike and Grim's Ditch, this low but immense linear feature offers views across London (to as far afield as Leith Hill in Surrey in good weather) although its origins are still mysterious.

In 1979 radiocarbon dating suggested that the dyke was in parts as much as two thousand years old, but much of it is thought to be merely fifth or sixth century. As such, the earthwork was perhaps not so much a defensive feature as a boundary marker, one dividing farmland belonging to Saxons from that of the local indigenous Britons. Now in parts densely wooded, it is also a reminder that the word 'weald' is of Saxon origin (meaning wood) and that much of the timber for Henry VII's breathtaking chapel at Westminster Abbey (see chapter 5) was felled in this part of Middlesex.

11. Burial Mounds

Greenwich Park, SE10

If one accepts the essentially pastoral nature of Saxon life it is tempting to imagine large areas of the old walled city being given over to pasture rather than being lived in, with some of the more extensive ruins perhaps providing makeshift stockades for sheep and cattle. Most of the population during this period preferred to live in small scattered Saxon settlements far beyond the walls, something we know from the number of familiar London place names that have clear Saxon origins.

Outlying villages such as Cynesigetun, Giseldone, Fulanhamme – 'a place of mud' – Lambehitha and Stybbanhyð coincide directly with modern Kensington, Islington, Fulham, Lambeth and Stepney. Similarly it is well away from the historic centre of London that one finds most of the burial grounds and barrows (or burial mounds) from the period, for example at Croydon and in the new Royal Borough of Greenwich, another name with clear Saxon origins.

In 1992 in Park Lane, Croydon a fourth-century burial ground was found to contain both cremation pots and graves, the site subsequently being preserved beneath an office car park. This rendered it safe from souvenir hunters, if impossible to see. In Greenwich Park, to the west of the Royal Observatory, visitors can clamber over the remains of more than forty barrows from the sixth and seventh centuries, although not all of these are any longer easy to discern.

Excavations of eighteen of the mounds in January 1784 produced a few coloured glass beads, some wool and auburn hair, a shield boss, a large iron spearhead and a knife. These seemed to indicate that the graves were pagan rather than Christian, a disappointment perhaps to the Reverend James Douglas who had led the expedition. Several of the tombs were also found to contain wooden coffins but without any bones still remaining.

The inevitable shortcomings of amateur eighteenth-century archaeologists such as Douglas mean it is still open to question whether these graves are Anglo-Saxon or Danish. But either way they are certainly of our period, and regardless of what happened to the bodies they provide another window onto these turbulent times. With successive waves of would-be invaders harrying not just the indigenous population but also the descendants of earlier immigrants, London was then as now very much a city in flux.

12. Crucifixion Scene

St Dunstan & All Saints, Stepney, E1

Built in the late tenth century by Dunstan, Bishop of London, the church of All Saints was renamed some time after Dunstan's canonization in 1029. Today it is largely a fifteenth-century building with nineteenth-century additions, but its history is clearly a long one, with the tenth-century structure thought to have replaced a wooden one that had already served the community for many decades, if not longer.

For our purposes its most interesting feature is a rare Anglo-Saxon rood at the east end of the church, the name given to a carved stone relief that would have formed part of a wooden screen used to divide the nave from the chancel in the original building. For many years the carving was assumed to be Norman, partly because of its slightly Romanesque decoration and because no other Saxon work had been found in the church. In fact it was correctly identified only as recently as 1988.

Rectangular, and approximately three feet by two, the grey limestone has been badly weathered (probably during a period when it was affixed to the outside of the church in the nineteenth century) but it clearly shows a finely carved crucifixion scene bordered by a robust leaf motif. Christ is shown with a halo in place, and beneath representations of the sun and moon the figures of the Virgin Mary and John the Baptist can be seen to be in deep mourning.

The Barnack stone from Cambridgeshire, and the style of the decoration, suggests it was carved some time after Dunstan's spell as Bishop of London (958–9) – perhaps following his appointment as Archbishop of Canterbury.

13. 'Grave of a Princess'

Floral Street, Covent Garden, WC2

As we saw in the previous chapter, more recent excavations have indicated the presence of a large Saxon settlement immediately to the west of Londinium. First mentioned as a port in a charter dated AD 672, by the mid-Saxon period the area around Covent Garden and stretching down to the river had grown into a thriving trading town.

The extent of this place, called Lundenwic, is still hard to gauge accurately, although a scattering of small finds point to it covering an area of around 150 acres by the time of the charter. It was to be relatively short-lived, however, and perhaps as a result of Viking raids in the mid-ninth century much of the area was returned to wasteland or farmland as the settlers wisely sought the protection of the walled city. Even then estimates of the population range no higher than ten to twelve thousand, so that by the time of the Norman conquest what we think of as London was still a substantially smaller place than Londinium had been more than six hundred years earlier.

However, finds associated with Lundenwic, while also mostly small, have not been without their highlights. In 2001, for example, a spectacular jewel 'fit for a princess' was discovered in a tomb on a construction site in Floral Street, Covent Garden. A beautiful disc brooch of copper and delicately worked gold, extremely finely crafted and studded with cabochon garnets from India, it is by far London's richest Saxon burial and has been compared to Suffolk's celebrated Sutton Hoo burial. Because of this, and with the same shallow grave yielding a quantity of beads and silver rings, archaeologists are confident that the incumbent, if not royal, would have been a member of the East Saxon nobility.

Five years earlier, again working ahead of the bulldozers and cranes on the site of the Royal Opera House, Covent Garden, another team of archaeologists had already uncovered evidence of several Saxon streets, houses and workshops. The Floral Street burial is therefore assumed to have been part of a graveyard, situated close to a small Saxon town that it would have served. More modest finds at the Jubilee Hall and in Maiden Lane, the result of so-called rescue archaeology, have tended to support this theory and the original location of Lundenwic. The remains of farm buildings have also been discovered beneath Trafalgar Square.

The subsequent retreat to the old Roman city makes a lot of sense, however, particularly given the ferocity of the Viking incursions that are known to have continued until as late as AD 994. The move also marked a crucial turning point for the history of London and its future development, and might also explain the derivation of the name of nearby Aldwych. Coming from the Saxon for 'old trading town', this description would make complete sense seen from the point of view of Saxons looking back at their old home from their 'new' town, safe from the Norsemen behind the Romans' old protective wall.

14. Queenhithe

Lower Thames Street, City of London, EC3

If the Stepney rood and All Hallows illustrate the Saxons' spirituality, it is necessary to follow the Saxons back into the City to find any evidence of commercial life during the later Saxon period.

It is clear that all the dispersed settlements, many of them probably just small clusters of relatively primitive houses, offered nothing to rival the thriving metropolis of Roman Londinium. Nevertheless by AD 731 the Venerable Bede, a scholarly monk frequently described as the father of English history, was able to describe a largish riverside community as 'a mart of many people coming by land and sea'.

At that time it is likely that many trading vessels were simply beached on the unembanked shore further upstream, where they could be safely unloaded between tides. But here at Queenhithe a more conventional quay was certainly in use and could be said to have laid the foundations of the modern city's financial and trading wealth.

The name itself is actually medieval, a reference to the unpopular Matilda of Scotland, Henry I's wife, who was granted the right in the early twelfth century to charge duties on any goods landed there. But, long before this, what is now thought to be the only surviving Saxon harbour in the world was known as Aedereshyd. It was a gift from Alfred the Great in AD 883 to his brother-in-law Ethelred (following his defeat of the Danes) and while much of it has been lost to development roughly half of the old rectangular harbour has survived for well over a thousand years.

It can be seen on the north bank of the river between Southwark and Blackfriars bridges, and as the last remaining inlet on the City waterfront it requires an intriguing little deviation in the course of the well-trodden Thames footpath. Incredibly it remained in use until well into the twentieth century (albeit by smaller vessels only) and in 1973 was finally declared a Scheduled Ancient Monument.

Sadly, work since then on vital flood defences means that nothing can now be seen of the original structure besides the basic outline of the harbour. Even so, it is extraordinary to think that well into the Middle Ages this relatively modest inlet was the most important harbour in the city, John Stow recording in 1603 that '*Ripa Regina*, the Queen's Bank or Hithe, may well be accounted the very chief and principal Water gate of this Citie.' Billingsgate, situated slightly further east and for centuries famous for its fish, was placed second.

Chapter 3

NORMAN LONDON

A truly decisive moment in English history – and by no means simply because it was, famously, the last successful invasion – 1066 saw the arrival of a people determined, unlike the Romans, to take what they wanted and to keep what they had conquered.

Indeed, so keen were they to impose on the natives their own customs and culture, their language, laws and institutions, that the Normans' enduring impact on the administration of London – and by extension life outside it for the general population – means that in the centuries following it becomes difficult if not impossible to see where the French influence ended and the English truly began.

15. The White Tower

Tower of London, EC3

This is still by far the most tangible and durable symbol of the Conqueror's hold on England and over the English. Very much the dominant feature of the Tower of London (and indeed in its day of London as a whole) the White Tower is not Britain's largest Norman keep – that honour belongs to Colchester Castle – but it is by far the most magnificent.

To reinforce the impression given of the new Norman supremacy, the stone was imported from Caen in France and the tall walls regularly whitewashed – hence the name. Even without this refinement, however, its immense bulk, rising ninety feet into the air, means it would have towered over the hovels and workshops of William's subjects to a far greater extent than even the largest Roman building.

Its construction was also very much a reaction to local hostility rather than an attempt to forestall it, a series of riots having followed William's coronation in Westminster Abbey on Christmas Day 1066, a deeply symbolic event from which the Saxon population had been expressly banned. The Normans perceived a need for what a contemporary chronicler describes as 'certain fortifications … against the fickleness of the vast and fierce population' and a suitable spot was quickly found on which work for such a structure could begin.

What is still technically a royal palace more than nine hundred years later was at first a relatively simple structure of wooden walls and defensive ditches, and evidence of the latter has been found suggesting that the original complex covered only slightly more than a single acre. But by 1077 Gandalf, Bishop of Rochester 'by command of King William the Great' was already at work 'supervising the work of the great tower of London', and it is his work that the visitor can see today.

In fact it is likely that the tower was still far from finished a decade later, when William died following a riding accident in 1087. But looking back this is neither here nor there, for even without the completed building the sheer scale of the work in hand would have been enough to awe most Londoners – exactly as intended.

With the benefit of hindsight the White Tower is also the most tangible reminder of William's sense of destiny. From the start his avowed intention had been for the Normans to remain in England, and that is how history was to play itself out. It was not until 1216 that this country finally had a king (Henry III) who had actually been born on native soil, not until Edward III (1327–77) that we had a king who spoke English, and of course even now much of the richness and variety of the English language still depends on that early injection of Norman French.

Today much of the interest for visitors to the White Tower depends on this intertwining of the two countries as much as it does on the building's antiquity. It is, for example, very much 'our' Tower of London in a way that, say, Hadrian's Wall is still viewed as something alien, an atmospheric but uncomfortable reminder of Britain's subjugation by a foreign enemy. The tower is also interesting because of its expressly multi-purpose role as a royal home, a prison, a garrison and armoury, and even for a while a menagerie or zoo.

Almost from the start it was intended to meet these many different needs, in particular the ceremonial and residential ones as well as the purely military. But, even knowing this, it comes as a surprise to step from outside and into St John's Chapel, from the military domain into the sacred, and into what remains the most original and most authentically Norman parts of the entire building.

The White Tower, after all, has stayed reasonably close to its builder's original intentions, but the appearance of the exterior is actually quite different as a number of typically narrow Norman windows were made larger in the eighteenth century. No such changes were ever made to the chapel, however, which – simple, austere and harmonious – is as a consequence as near-perfect an example of early Norman church architecture as one could hope to find anywhere.

With its rounded arches, simple, stocky stone columns, and sturdy, robust groin vaults, it is a very pure expression of the early Normans' architectural ideal. This makes it seem a more natural and somehow more organic composition than later buildings incorporating the soaring and technically ingenious pointed arches that came to define the Gothic in later centuries; also one with a hewn-from-the-solid feel, which perhaps better than any other conveys the energy and force with which the Normans recast England in their own image.

It may once have been painted in bright colours, but now with little in the way of decoration or adornment, and a style that seems to celebrate the virtue of simplicity, it is to be counted among the most bewitching of London interiors from literally any era.

16. Thomas à Becket's Birthplace

Cheapside, City of London, EC2

Inevitably, over time, the lines of demarcation began to blur between the invader and the invaded. For a very long time the elite were essentially still Normans, but a process of mingling gradually began to erode the boundaries to the point where it becomes hard – perhaps even irrelevant – to ask whether a particular individual was English or French.

One suspects that St Thomas à Becket (*c.*1118–70) is someone who most people today regard as an Englishman and an English saint, a martyred Archbishop of Canterbury who unusually is revered by both Anglicans and Roman Catholics. It is true that he was born on English soil, in a house on Cheapside in the City of London (the site is now occupied by a shoe shop selling, appropriately, men's footwear under the brand name Church's). He was educated in part here too, at Merton Priory in what was then Surrey, but which today is a London borough straddling the Northern Line.

His antecedents were nevertheless entirely French. Before settling in London his father, Gilbert Becket, was a merchant and small landowner from Thierville in the lordship of Brionne (in what is now Haute-Normandie). His mother, Matilda, was also Norman, and not as is often supposed a Saracen princess who made eyes at Gilbert while he made a pilgrimage to the Holy Land. As this suggests, her true origins are still somewhat uncertain, but probably coming from Caen (like the Conqueror) she is thought to have been related to Archbishop Theobald of Canterbury, a connection that the family pursued while seeking to obtain a position for young Thomas.

Becket entered Theobald's service in 1145, and after working as his secretary and confidential agent was soon rewarded with Canterbury's valuable archdeaconry before returning to London as Henry II's chancellor. This was an impressive rise in status for a young man, but one entirely in keeping with the Norman elite's wish to ensure that the levers of power remained in the hands of Frenchmen, or at least those with clear and close French connections.

Highly talented when it came to matters of finance, administration, politics and diplomacy, Becket soon amassed a fortune, which he clearly enjoyed to the full (his personal lifestyle was always considered to be more lavish than his sovereign's). Showing an apparent willingness to side with the Crown rather than the Church, his preferment now seemed assured and in 1162 he was duly enthroned at Canterbury, the first non-monk to be appointed Archbishop having been ordained as a priest only hours earlier.

The remainder of the story is well known. As primate Becket very quickly adopted a markedly more ascetic lifestyle, resigning the chancellorship and – while Henry expected him to continue putting the needs of Crown and State ahead of the Church – making moves to claw back powers which, he felt, Canterbury had unwisely relinquished in previous years.

This meant opposing the king, of course, which Becket now seemed to do at every turn, in particular by attempting to remove churchmen from the authority of the courts. Following a famous if almost certainly fictionalized exhortation to be rid of 'this turbulent priest' (or 'low-born cleric', accounts differ), Henry subsequently learnt that the challenge had been taken up by four knights, and that Becket had been cut down and killed in his own cathedral on 29 December 1170.

Once again myth piled on top of legend, and the inevitable rewriting of history means that the details of his murder are unlikely ever to be known for certain. What is known is that the four knights had to cross the Channel in order to do the king's bidding, and that – like St Thomas à Becket, and indeed Henry II – they were, essentially, French.

17. St Mary Magdalene

Norman Road, East Ham, E15

Contrasting strongly with the Chapel of St John, a place of kings within the Tower of London, St Mary Magdalene is a simple parish church. It is of a broadly similar age, however, and – but for a sixteenth-century tower and a small entrance porch – it still conforms to the basic three-part arrangement that worshippers would have expected to find in 1130: that is, an aisleless nave, a narrow chancel and a sanctuary. Because of this, and a large churchyard, and despite its proximity to extensive public housing schemes and Sir Joseph Bazalgette's immense mid-Victorian Northern Outfall Sewer, it still looks very much like the little country church it once was.

A Saxon charter describes a place called Hamme in 958, meaning an area of dry land between rivers or marshes, and in 1086 Hame is mentioned in *Domesday* when it would still have been a hamlet many miles from London. In Bazalgette's time the community was still described as a 'scattered village', and indeed it was not until 1965 that it was finally incorporated into a borough, named London Borough of Newham.

39

Given all this, the survival in such good shape of what is in essence still a country church is indeed quite remarkable. (This is especially so as this must have been quite a prosperous village at some point in its history, meaning that, for whatever reason, the impulse to rebuild or 'improve' must have been resisted.)

The impression one gets on entering St Mary Magdalene is thus overwhelmingly one of entering a Norman building. As with the White Tower, some of the window openings have been enlarged slightly but many of the roof timbers are original and some are still held together using twelfth-century wooden pegs. Similarly, while the builders employed a variety of different materials – including the by now familiar Kentish ragstone, as well as finer quality Caen stone and recycled Roman tiles – the mortar used to bind them is a known Norman recipe, which one can assume was mixed and applied by Norman craftsmen.

Inside on the north wall is a short run of blind arcading – the shape of the feature's intersecting arches, the rough workmanship and the simple zig-zag decoration giving away its Norman origins. The same can be said for the moulding around the west doorway, which now leads into the tower. A form of decoration that is rare enough in properly rural churches, this is a really astonishing thing to stumble upon in twenty-first-century London.

18. The Clerk's Well

Farringdon Lane, Clerkenwell, EC1

While the derivation of the name Clerkenwell has long been understood, the actual well was lost and presumed destroyed until it was discovered during building work in the 1920s.

What can be seen now (by arrangement with Islington Borough Council) is on the whole Tudor brickwork, but the well itself is evidently much older and was certainly in use during the Norman period. William Fitzstephen, a clerk employed by Thomas à Becket, mentions several such wells in his 'Descriptio Nobilissimi Civitatis Londoniae' (A Description of the Noble City of London) dated not later than 1180 – describing how mysteries or religious dramas were performed by London clerks and lower clergy who gathered around this particular one.

The well was still in use nearly six hundred years later, historian John Strype in 1720 locating it on the road from Clerkenwell to Hockley-in-the-Hole. Around 1800 it was at last replaced by a pump, however, and eventually it fell into disuse though possibly no earlier than the mid-nineteenth century. Infilled with rubbish at this point, and then built over, its location remained lost until 1924. The delightful-sounding Hockley-in-the-Hole, incidentally, would have been slightly to the north of the junction of Farringdon Road and Clerkenwell Road.

19. St Bartholomew the Great*

Smithfield, EC1

Although a very large city church, what we see now is only a tiny portion of Smithfield's long vanished Augustinian house, the Priory of St Bartholomew, whose own nave was an extraordinary 280 feet in length.

The priory had been founded in 1123 by Rahere – a monk, prebendary to St Paul's and a leading figure in the court of Henry I. Falling dangerously ill while returning from a pilgrimage to Rome, Rahere received a vision of St Bartholomew and promised – were he lucky enough to survive long enough to return to London – to found the priory and the neighbouring hospital, which still bears the Apostle's name.

The priory was completed around 1145 but then shared the fate of others like it during the reign of

* St Bartholomew-the-Less is close by, within the precincts of Bart's Hospital.

Henry VIII, when the great nave was mostly torn down. Unusually a few parts of the monastic complex were left intact, and new uses found for some of the smaller buildings, perhaps as a consequence of their convenient location right on London's boundary. Whatever the reason, the canons' choir and sanctuary also survived, and were soon in use as a normal parish church. Another survivor was the famous Bartholomew Fair – the canons had been granted by Henry I the rights to hold this – although this was eventually suppressed in 1855 when the associated revels became too rowdy.

Today the surviving portion of the monks' church can be identified by its pointed arches, conceivably the oldest of this type in London, although many more traditional round-headed arches at ground and first-floor level (and several huge circular pillars) betray the church's exceptionally early date. Clearly these simple forms lack the soaring, more poetic quality of later, pointed Gothic architecture but, as previously described, the simplicity and solidity of the largely plain stonework seems to exemplify the powerful, no-nonsense, plain-speaking qualities we have come to associate with the Conqueror and his descendants.

One other feature of the church is also of note, and that is the gateway that leads on to the street known as Little Britain. Like the rest of the church, which fell largely into disuse in the mid-1800s, this was heavily restored by Sir Aston Webb towards the end of that century. The upper portions are half-timbered and decidedly picturesque, particularly when seen from the churchyard, but the gateway beneath is thirteenth century. It marks the position of the western entrance to the aforementioned nave, thereby giving the visitor something of an impression of its immense length.

20. Temple Church

off Middle Temple Lane, City of London, EC4

With hindsight it is too easy and perhaps unfair to fault the work of nineteenth-century restorers, when many of them (including Webb at St Bartholomew's) had honest motives but often had poor material to work with. Some deserve the criticisms levelled at them, however, and too often buildings have suffered irreparably at their hands. Here for example, at what for many visitors is the capital's most 'famously Norman' Norman church, much if not all of the mystery and magic of a twelfth-century building is entirely missing. The reason for this is not hard to discern, and is perhaps best expressed in the words of the architectural historian Walter Godfrey describing how 'every ancient surface was repaired away or renewed'.

The work started early, with Wren adding battlements in the 1680s and the Victorians carrying out what were termed repairs. Much of these were then eradicated during the Blitz, when the magnificent east window was destroyed and many of the crusaders' tombs badly damaged. Fortunately the original Norman ground plan survived intact through it all and, because of this (and its relatively secluded location), London's only round church (one of only four in England) is still an extraordinary and rewarding place to visit.

The builders were the Knights Templar, a much storied order that was established in the eleventh century expressly to protect pilgrims on their way to Jerusalem. More formally known as the *Pauperes commilitones Christi Templique Salomonici* (Poor Fellow-Soldiers of Christ and of the Temple of Solomon), the knights rapidly established themselves as an effective fighting force for the Crusades and an economic powerhouse as alms and bequests were showered on them. Very soon they had a presence in many European countries, including France, Aragon, Portugal, Hungary and Croatia – and in England its members were well established in this part of London by the reign of Henry I.

Their first church was completed around 1162 in Holborn, but as early as 1185 it was replaced by the building we see today, which at that time would have formed part of a larger monastic complex known as the

New Temple. The unusual circular design was almost certainly modelled not on Jerusalem's Church of the Holy Sepulchre (as is normally said) but on the Dome of the Rock, a building of immense historical and religious significance for Jews, Christians and Muslims alike.

With the monks owning even more land on the south side of the river, by the thirteenth century it was a magnificent establishment and one that played host to kings and papal grandees (King John was staying here when he was summoned to sign the Magna Carta in the presence of the barons). Inevitably such great wealth aroused envy and distrust, and in the fourteenth century the order was entirely discredited after Pope Clement had been persuaded to withdraw Rome's support and suppress the knights.

The charges against them – of blasphemy, sodomy, heresy and even usury (as they were by this time successful bankers) – were probably in the main false, but in London (as elsewhere) the knights were arrested and imprisoned and their property forfeit. Thereafter, and in a manner that was not entirely straightforward, the church and the land around it eventually came into the possession of London's lawyers, who still have the freeholds today. Controversial if on the whole caring custodians, the Inns of Court at least nurture their peaceful inner-city enclaves, and during business hours the public are able to enjoy much of what they offer.

Chapter 4

MEDIEVAL LONDON

The medieval city was a large and thriving metropolis, some six or seven times larger than its nearest English rivals, Norwich and York. A successful and prosperous trading centre, the walled city was ringed by a number of hugely wealthy monastic foundations and it was through these that new styles in art and architecture arrived in England to be gradually absorbed into English culture.

For London and Britain generally it was something of a golden era, and yet today, if there is a single defining image of medieval life, it is one of the many gruesome and frightening scenes from the Black Death. This global pandemic is said to have killed around one-third of the population of England and as many as thirty thousand Londoners.

These are just guesses – accurate numbers are impossible to gauge – although it is known that the population of London took 150 years to return to its pre-plague level of around seventy thousand people. It is also known that, by the winter of 1348, city graveyards were literally overflowing, and that new mass graves were soon being excavated around the city walls.

These included one at Grey Friars (to the north of St Paul's) and another on more than a dozen acres near Smithfield,* land bought expressly for this purpose by the benefactor Sir Walter de Manny, a knight of Edward III's and founder of the adjacent Charterhouse.

21. The Killing Fields

Old Spitalfields Market, E1

So numerous were London's plague pits that the tendency now is to assume that any large common grave found any-where in the city dates from this period. It was therefore something of a surprise to many when archaeologists

---

* In the spring of 2013 it was announced that workers engaged in the Crossrail scheme had found the remains of thirteen plague victims in Charterhouse Street. Described as a 'rare and important find' this brought the total number of bodies recovered as a result of the Crossrail project to more than three hundred, with a further four thousand bodies from the fourteenth to seventeenth centuries expected to come to light when work began closer to Liverpool Street Station on the site of the old Bedlam Hospital.

from the Museum of London published their findings in 2012 showing that one of the largest – on the site of a vanished Augustinian priory and the hospital of St Mary Spital – was far older. Unexpectedly, the survey also found that many of the more than 10,500 bodies buried on the site were victims not of plague but of famine.

A lengthy bioarchaeological study of several thousand of the remains, including radiocarbon dating, pointed to a date of 1258. The cause of the famine was soon traced to a gigantic volcanic eruption on the other side of the world, a blast so powerful that it reduced temperatures around the world by sending millions of tons of ash and other debris up into the atmosphere.

Contemporary accounts describe a period of serious climate change occurring at the start of that year. Matthew Paris, for example, the monk and early chronicler of English history, describes how 'the north wind blew without intermission, a continued frost prevailed, accompanied by snow and such unendurable cold, that it bound up the face of the earth and sorely afflicted the poor'. In particular, he writes, the big chill 'suspended all cultivation, and killed the young of the cattle to such an extent that it seemed as if a general plague was raging amongst the sheep and lambs'.

The impact on the population in the capital, particularly those he characterizes as coming from the lower orders, was entirely as expected, which is to say appalling.

The famine, says Paris, 'spread death among them in a most lamentable degree' – with as many as fifteen thousand Londoners dying of starvation and tens of thousands dying elsewhere in the country.

Even now it is not known where precisely the volcanic eruption occurred, with candidates including Mexico, Ecuador and Indonesia. The mechanics of the calamity are well understood, however, as a sufficient volume of ash in the atmosphere can very quickly reduce temperatures around the world by a critical four degrees centigrade or more. Temperatures globally are known to have been affected in this way for several years following the famous Krakatoa eruption of 1883, and the evidence of ice core samples in Antarctica suggests that the eruption that precipitated London's first great medieval disaster – wherever the eruption took place – may have been as much as eight times more powerful.

22. Effigy of a Knight

Southwark Cathedral, London Bridge, SE1

Many of those ranked above Paris's 'lower orders' escaped the worst effects of the famine, and most could expect a better end than being tipped into a mass grave. One such is the recumbent knight who can be found in the north choir aisle of Southwark Cathedral, itself a medieval gem that is all too often overlooked.

The origins of this riverside spot as a religious site are seventh century or older, but somewhat mysterious: the most popular legend is that the first church was paid for by a ferryman who enriched himself at a time before a bridge was built linking Southwark and London.

More certain is that the Cathedral Church of St Saviour and St Mary Overie is the third replacement for the ferryman's original bequest, and that with a foundation date of around 1220 it is London's earliest surviving Gothic church. It was built to replace a Norman building (part of a twelfth-century Augustinian priory, largely destroyed by fire in 1212) and although much altered in the fourteenth, seventeenth and nineteenth centuries the present cathedral still boasts some of the finest examples of early English work in the country.

Inside it is hard to miss the contrast with the heavy Norman columns, as previously described. In place of the simple but robust circular pillars of the Chapel of St John (see chapter 3, St Mary Magdalene), here the stone roof of the retrochoir seems almost to float above

the floor, a gloriously complex but unadorned canopy of pointed arches that is held aloft by slender, beautifully worked columns. It is still a relatively simple interior, with decoration kept to a minimum; but gazing up one can somehow sense the pleasure that the craftsmen employed here must have taken in their newly acquired skills and self-evident technical mastery.

The same can probably be said for the man who carved this effigy of a knight, around 1275, although like the ferryman – and indeed the knight – his identity remains unknown. Work of this sort is sadly very rare in London, a city where – with the notable exception of Westminster Abbey – sculpture from this period has on the whole fared badly (this abbey has enjoyed the protection due to a Royal Peculiar, a church that comes under the direct control of the sovereign rather than a diocese).

At St Paul's an astonishingly rich collection was lost in the Great Fire; the Blitz caused immense damage to the effigies of various knights arranged around the circular nave of the Temple Church; and elsewhere a combination of neglect and wilful destruction has devastated what would otherwise have been a priceless cultural legacy. But here at least something of the Middle Ages has survived, and this idealized image of a nobleman in blackened oak (one of fewer than one hundred such wooden effigies in the country) conforms exactly to our notions of the Age of Chivalry.

With his face at peace, his legs crossed and a mailed hand grasping a sword, the knight's name may be lost but a possible connection has been made with a family called de Warenne. They had strong connections with this area, but in the absence of any heraldic embellishments, which tended to be employed later, even this cannot be confirmed.

Nearby another carving, this time in stone, explores that other great medieval obsession – with death. This is a *gisant*, a French term describing a representation of a dying man or emaciated corpse – a shrouded, decomposing figure celebrating the ugly torments of death in a way that today seems extraordinarily gruesome (largely because it is). Rather easier on the eye is the cathedral's third treasure, John Gower's memorial. A friend and contemporary of Chaucer's, and a poet himself who died in 1408, he is depicted with his head resting on three of his best-known volumes: *Speculum Hominis, Vox Clamantis* and *Confessio Amantis*.

23. Eltham Palace

Eltham, Royal Borough of Greenwich, SE9

With its vitrolite tiling, sweeping circular hall and advanced technologies such as piped music and centralized vacuum cleaning, the 1930s creation of textile heir Stephen Courtauld and his wife Virginia may be English Heritage's most magnificent twentieth-century showpiece but Eltham Palace has a history dating back nearly a thousand years.

Originally granted to Odo, William the Conqueror's half-brother, this was an important royal residence throughout much of the Middle Ages and, despite its breathtaking art deco flourishes, it is still technically part of the Crown Estate.

In 1305 it was given to the future Edward II, the first ever Prince of Wales if one discounts a handful of Welsh warlords (who adopted the title in earlier centuries without the authority or permission of the English Crown). His queen, Isabella, spent much of her time at Eltham Palace along with their son (the future Edward III) and records show that by 1359 as much as £2,000 had been spent on improvements, an astonishing sum for the time. For a while the clerk of works was Geoffrey Chaucer, and improvements continued to be carried out here until well into the sixteenth century.

As all this suggests, medieval Eltham was, and in part remains, a singularly impressive place, with an inner court for the king, his family and closest associates and an outer one for the functionaries and those charged with maintaining security. Popularly supposed to be where Edward III founded the 'Order of the Blue

Garter' – today's Most Noble Order of the Garter – it is also where King John II of France was received after being captured and brought to England. Henry VIII spent much of his childhood here too, although his daughter Elizabeth was never more than an occasional visitor and thereafter Eltham seems to have fallen out of favour.

Reported to be 'much out of repair' by the time of Charles I's execution it was sold to an officer of the Parliamentarian army who began to demolish it and died leaving behind a ruin. Fortunately the great hall survived, albeit as a barn, its most impressive feature being a vast medieval hammerbeam roof. London's largest great hall – excepting Westminster Hall, which has the largest medieval wooden roof anywhere in Europe – this is of such quality that in the 1820s Sir Jeffry Wyattville considered removing it to use as part of his extensions to Windsor Castle.

Having had such a narrow escape it seems extraordinary now that a century later the authorities were happy to lease it to a wealthy couple, knowing they had plans to extend and modify such an obviously important building. That said, the Courtaulds' new house is an undeniable triumph, arguably the best country house interior of the period anywhere in England, and given the fate of so many other medieval structures in and around London their tenure of Eltham Palace may well have saved one of the few decent secular buildings we have left.

24. Black Prince Pub

Kennington, SE11

In 1337 Edward III gave the manor of Kennington to his son Edward of Woodstock, the victor of Crécy who was better known as the Black Prince and is commemorated in the name of this inner-city boozer.

Edward built a large royal palace close to the road junction known as Kennington Cross, but nearly seven hundred years later nothing of this remains although, remarkably, the land on which it stood continues to be passed down to successive generations of royal heirs. Today it forms an important part of the Duchy of Cornwall, around forty acres of inner London being included in the valuable inheritance that the present Prince of Wales enjoys as Duke of Cornwall.

The Black Prince, a formidable military leader who captured and ransomed King John II of France, was also the first ever Knight of the Garter (in 2008 Prince William became the thousandth, making this the world's oldest order of chivalry still extant). Details of his palace are sketchy, however, although it is known that by 1363 it included a new hall, a 'Prince's Chamber' and other chambers, a wardrobe, new kitchens, a bakehouse and a dwelling for a pastry cook.

Such domestic details might disguise what was by any reckoning a decidedly princely establishment, the great hall being entirely of stone and measuring approximately eighty-eight feet long by fifty-three feet wide, and the Prince's Chamber scarcely any smaller. Its cost was put at a huge sum of £1,845 5*s* 5*d*, an almost incalculable amount in today's currency.

A convenient refuge from London, it was a favourite of Richard II's and remained in use as an occasional royal residence until the reign of Henry Tudor as Henry VII before, in 1531, it was largely torn down to provide materials for Henry VIII's new Whitehall Palace. Thereafter, Charles I is known to have lived on part of the site prior to his accession to the throne, but today the Prince of Wales – while a notably good landlord – is only ever a visitor.

25. Plague Pit

East Smithfield, Tower Hamlets, E1

London's mass graves and plague pits, while clearly numerous, seem sometimes to be outnumbered by the legends that surround them. For example, that a seventeenth-century lad fell into one of them and was forced to gnaw on the bones to sustain himself before they pulled him out. That the basements at Harvey Nichols are shallower than normal because this was thought preferable to digging out all the corpses. And that work on the Victoria Line in the 1960s had to stop temporarily when a tunnelling machine beneath Green Park began to grind up hundreds of human bones after unexpectedly hitting an old plague pit.

It is similarly said that there are more dead bodies in the non-conformist Bunhill Fields cemetery off Old Street than living in the whole of Southampton – although this could actually be correct, and the name really is a derivation of 'Bone Hill'. It is also known that during the plague itself two chancellors and three Archbishops of Canterbury all died in very quick succession, and it is

likely that the large black slab in the Westminster Abbey cloisters conceals remains of the abbot and more than two dozen of his monks who also succumbed.

In all probability we will never know the true number of deaths, but genuine plague pits are still being discovered on a fairly regular basis and they can provide a fascinating glimpse into these turbulent years of London history. In the 1980s, for example, excavations at East Smithfield, between the buildings of the old Royal Mint and the Tower of London, at first revealed a fairly orderly pattern of burials – that is, more like a conventional graveyard. But a further more detailed examination of the bones quickly established that the bodies were associated with a single catastrophe, the Black Death, and not with the normal mortality patterns for Middle Age London.

With bodies stacked five deep, the find provided an important opportunity to study plague victims' bodies in the greatest detail, and to date East Smithfield is the most fully analysed site of its kind anywhere in Europe.

In part, the greater than normal interest in the site came about because it was thought that 'dental pulp' from the skeletons could in some way come to the aid of modern medical science (possibly even in the treatment of HIV, as a mutant gene that offers some immunity to this is now believed to have its origins in the Black Death). Scientists from home and abroad were also keen to sequence the genome of the bubonic plague itself, hoping that it would prove possible to track changes in the evolution and virulence of the pathogen over time.

Unfortunately it has so far remained unclear what renders the disease quite so deadly – extraordinarily it still kills approximately two thousand people per year globally – but almost certainly it is this knowledge that a mass killer lurks unseen in the soil of modern London that explains the fascination we still have for plague pits, whether they be lost, found, real or imagined.

26. An Old Brown Shoe

Thames foreshore, Billingsgate, City of London, EC3

Skeletons and effigies can say a lot about life in the past, providing the kind of information that even the best contemporary accounts and memoirs leave out. But sometimes the most evocative details come from the simplest objects, household items lost or discarded in the street, many of which – like a broken fourteenth-century leather shoe that is now in the Museum of London – eventually found their way into the city's great open sewer, the Thames.

For latterday mudlarks, the licensed descendants of the bands of Victorian scavengers who used to eke out a poor living along the shore at low tide, there are potentially rich pickings to be had. Finds pulled from the ooze have included the remains of a pair of twelfth-century ice skates, a variety of different weapons, some primitive spectacles made around 1440 and – by far the most valuable – a magnificent Plantagenet collar of interlocking solid silver links.

The most poignant, however, is perhaps this shoe. It is just one of a surprising quantity of footwear to have survived, enough in fact for us to know as much about medieval Londoners' feet as we do about any other parts of their bodies. It turns out that their feet were smaller than our own, but not by much, and that they suffered as much as we do with the same run of corns and more serious deformities such as arthritic, hammer and pigeon toes.

The owner of this shoe had a huge bunion on the right side of his left foot, sufficiently large to wear a hole right through the shoe (this can be clearly seen). We can also surmise that his affliction was made even more uncomfortable by the fourteenth-century fashion for wearing shoes too narrow for the feet they were intended to enclose.

Even without peering too long at the replica foot on display in the Museum of London (complete with its repulsive, swelling *hallux abducto valgus*) it is easy to share in the fashion victim's discomfort, and to imagine the pain he must have experienced while walking uphill from the river towards St Paul's. This perhaps is what gives the shoe its strong narrative punch, allowing a glimpse into a life long extinguished and a reminder that modern Londoners and their medieval counterparts are really not that far apart.

27. Whitefriars' Priory

Magpie Alley, Fleet Street, EC4

The depredations of Henry VIII mean that today it is hard to appreciate not just the wealth and influence of English medieval religious foundations but also the size of the many monasteries, priories, convents and friaries that crowded the streets of the capital before the Dissolution (1536–41).

Their churches alone give a good indication as to the scale of these immense, self-contained communities. For example, the one belonging to the Black Friars (so named because of the black cloak or *cappa* that the Augustinians wore over their white habits) was 220 feet in length. The White Friars' was 260 feet, the Austin Friars' 265 feet, and the Grey Friars' closer to 300 feet, with the nave of modern St Paul's, for comparison, a mere 223 feet.

Yet today, of all of them, almost nothing remains beyond street names and the odd lonely isolated fragment.

Most of the buildings were sacked on the orders of Henry VIII or sold off, and the few buildings that survived to be used for other purposes mostly fell in the Great Fire or were subsequently torn down.

Very occasionally a lost piece of brick or stonework comes to light, but it is extraordinary how the destruction was so total as to leave barely a trace. In 1890 a small stone arcade was discovered in Blackfriars and re-erected at the Bishop of Rochester's home near Croydon. A few years later some more fragments were removed to St Dominic's Priory between Hampstead and Camden. For a while it looked as if the only monastic buildings to survive would be those of the Grey Friars in Newgate Street, which in 1553 were given to Christ's Hospital (a school). These buildings remained standing for the next 350 years, but when the pupils were relocated to Sussex in 1902 they too were demolished to make way for a new General Post Office.

All this means that today the only really tangible monastic survivor is this modest chalk-block crypt in an alleyway off Fleet Street. Originally it would have formed a small, very unimportant part of the Whitefriars' priory, a community with origins on Mount Carmel (Carmelite Street is near to the priory) and who arrived in London in 1241 after being driven out of the Holy Land by the Saracens.

Those early monks, popular with the people of London and quickly attracting many rich patrons – including John of Gaunt – occupied a site that stretched from Fleet Street to the Thames, and from what is now Whitefriars Street all the way to the Temple. Following the Dissolution most of their buildings fell into disrepair and became workshops or mean dwellings, and the crypt, in reality never more than a small undercroft, was used as a coal cellar before becoming effectively lost to the world.

The refectory, or great hall, was eventually converted into a playhouse, and Ben Jonson was one of several leading dramatists who produced works to be performed here by a company called the Children of the Queen's Revels. By 1630, however, nothing was left standing above ground and the story might have ended there but for the chance discovery towards the end of the nineteenth century of a section of pavement thought to have come from the monks' cloister.

Further investigations during redevelopment work suggested that the coal cellar beneath a rundown property in Britton's Court was actually many hundreds of years older than was thought, and steps were taken to preserve it. Later still, more building in the area meant that it had to be moved a few yards, and today it is displayed behind glass in the basement of a firm of lawyers backing on to Magpie Alley.

It is not possible to enter the crypt, or to walk around it, and it is too dark to get anything more than a glimpse of the interior from outside. But the crypt is safe, and having been carefully restored in the 1920s it is now securely mounted on a concrete base that was installed during the relocation.

28. Winchester Palace

Clink Street, Southwark, SE1

Close to Tower Bridge, the lofty if fragmentary remains of a bishop's palace must rank as one of London's most surprising survivors, a portion of a great medieval hall – complete with a large and elegant rose window – which, thought lost, was discovered by accident following a huge warehouse fire in 1814.

The original palace was Norman, and according to Thomas à Becket's earliest biographer it was where the martyr spent his last night before his murder in Canterbury. Thereafter the building remained in use until the mid-seventeenth century, latterly as a prison, the great hall now known to be a fourteenth-century extension completed at a time when the bishops of Winchester were still a powerful force in the country.

With many castles and estates across the south of England, the bishops frequently played host to English and continental royalty, and some idea of the size and magnificence of the hall can be assumed from the knowledge that it was where James I of Scotland chose to have his wedding feast in 1424. More than eighty feet in length, and half as broad, it is also thought to be where Henry VIII first encountered Catherine Howard, his fifth wife.

Confiscated during the Commonwealth, and unfortunately heavily dilapidated by the time it was returned at the Restoration, a decision was soon after taken to develop the site. Thereafter the area became notorious for its gaming, gambling and brothels (one hopes to the embarrassment of the bishops, as this part of Southwark still fell under their jurisdiction not the City of London's) and at some point the parts of the building we see today were incorporated into new warehousing, which spread along this stretch of the Thames.

In 1814 one of the warehouses was let to a company of mustard makers, and that summer a disastrous fire coincided with a low tide that prevented 'fire floats' from playing their hoses onto the flames. The damage inflicted over several hours was extensive, but once under control the south wall of the old hall was revealed together with the west gable end and its magnificent thirteen-foot rose window.

Chapter 5

TUDOR LONDON

Beginning with the Tudor accession in 1485, and before their rapid expansion was momentarily reversed by the plague and then the Great Fire, the twin cities of London and Westminster underwent a period of incredible growth. With the population of the capital quadrupling in a little over a century (to about two hundred thousand strong by 1600) England's pre-eminence in global trading, and the development of former monastic properties following the Dissolution, began the process of transforming London into the world city it is today.

The growth of the metropolis was such that already Londoners were complaining about the disappearance of the green fields of their youth, and the diarist John Evelyn was not alone in noting that the population had doubled in his own lifetime.

Perhaps the most obvious change this brought was that the city finally and irrevocably broke out beyond the old Roman and medieval walls. The expansion was far from planned or orderly; instead London grew by fits and starts as isolated settlements outside the walls – and beyond the ring of monasteries – expanded to connect with or absorb each other. The destruction by Henry VIII of the monasteries hastened the spread by freeing up yet more land while providing a useful supply of salvaged building material and creating a new class of property developer in the aristocrats and others who had been gifted the abandoned buildings by their rapacious sovereign – or had bought them.

29. Henry VII Chapel

Westminster Abbey, SW1

Exemplifying the era's wealth, power and cultural sophistication, with its breathtaking fan-vaulted ceiling and exceptionally delicate carved tracery, Henry Tudor's extension to Westminster Abbey is frequently described as the single most important architectural achievement in Tudor London.

Set apart from the main body of the abbey by splendid

brass gates and a flight of stone steps, it can very easily be seen (if not quite dismissed) as a cynical exercise in legitimizing the Tudor claim to the throne. Following the Plantagenet defeat it was always Henry's intention to create a new royal mausoleum for his fledgling dynasty, and by doing this at Westminster he had certainly alighted on a place of the deepest symbolic significance to the English Crown and English people.

It was also a sincere exercise in piety, however, being both a shrine to Henry VI (whom Henry VII expected to be canonized) and entirely in keeping with the fashion at the time for consecrating lady chapels dedicated to the Virgin Mary. But, as it happened, there was to be no English St Henry until long after the builder's death, and so Henry VII and his wife eventually came to occupy the central tomb themselves, with numerous other royal interments taking place in the chapel in the decades that followed.

The complexity of the architecture and the quality of the craftsmanship means that the interior took many years to complete, and it was far from finished at the time of Henry's death in 1509. The task of seeing the job through to its conclusion thus fell to his son, a strange turn of events given Henry VIII's justifiable reputation as a destroyer rather than a creator of large and important religious buildings. Yet at least it was Henry VIII's father who was paying for the work, Henry VII having set aside

£14,000 for this during his lifetime and allocating half as much again in his will. (The total might thus be equivalent to £120 million or more in today's terms, although at such a distance such calculations are notoriously fraught and almost certainly unreliable.)

It was afterwards said that the late king was more finely accommodated dead than he had been when alive, and looking at other buildings of the period this could well be true, for in every way the chapel is quite exceptional. There was also an understanding that no one but the bluest of blue bloods should be accorded the honour of a burial alongside him, and following the Restoration most of those who were not of royal descent were exhumed and quietly buried elsewhere.

The unsurprising exception to this gentle manner of relocation was the despised Oliver Cromwell, who having somewhat curiously modelled his own funeral on that of James I also determined that he should afterwards be buried alongside him in the chapel. In 1661, however, Cromwell was rudely disinterred and posthumously beheaded together with several other regicides. For the next quarter of a century his head was to remain on a pole outside Westminster Hall, a gruesome relic displayed by the entrance to the historic site.

30. Fulham Palace

Bishop's Avenue, SW6

More of a manor house than a palace, this episcopal pile of around 1510 is one of several attractive Tudor country houses that now find themselves slightly marooned well inside the boundaries of greater London. Others include Eastbury in Barking, Hall Place in Bexleyheath and Eltham's Tudor Barn (actually the surviving portion of moated Well Hall, home to Sir John Pulteney who was four times London's Lord Mayor).

At each of them the overwhelming impression is of pleasantly mellow Tudor brick, and at least externally Fulham is no exception to this, although most of its interiors are Georgian and its origins in reality far older. In fact, records show that the site has been owned by the bishops for more than 1,300 years, and from the eighteenth century until as recently as 1975 the palace served as their principal residence.

One late seventeenth-century bishop, Henry Compton, keen to enhance more than thirty acres of gardens imported several rare species of tree, many of which still stand. (Another of his imports was a Dutch king,

Compton helping to promote the Glorious Revolution by inviting William of Orange to seize the throne from Catholic James II.) The grounds were later given over to allotments during the Second World War, when the palace sustained some light damage, and like the palace these are open to the public throughout the week, and at no charge.

31. The Chapel Royal of St Peter ad Vincula

Tower of London, EC3

With such a long history the Tower of London necessarily includes architecture of many ages and styles, and this small but special church within its walls is an exceptionally fine example of Perpendicular Gothic.

The name means St Peter in Chains, an appropriate dedication for a church whose fate it has been to provide the final resting places for many of those who lost their heads on the adjacent Tower Green. Not all were traitors, some merely fell foul of their sovereign, but among the most famous are the Tudor queens – Anne Boleyn, Catherine Howard and Lady Jane Grey who reigned for just nine days in 1553. But as well as Lady

Jane's husband, Lord Guilford Dudley, the bodycount includes a trio of Catholic saints – Thomas More, John Fisher and the 20th Earl of Arundel – together with Thomas Cromwell and the dukes of Northumberland, Somerset and Suffolk.

All had been men of power and influence, but in turbulent times each in some way offended the ruling Tudors and paid the maximum price for doing so. Thomas Macauly, visiting the church in the 1840s for his popular *History of England*, observed that there was 'no sadder spot in England'. Here, he said, death is associated 'not, as in Westminster Abbey and Saint Paul's, with genius and virtue, with public veneration and with imperishable renown; not, as in our humblest churches and churchyards, with everything that is most endearing in social and domestic charities; but with whatever is darkest in human nature and in human destiny, with the savage triumph of implacable enemies, with the inconstancy, the ingratitude, the cowardice of friends, with all the miseries of fallen greatness and of blighted fame'.

He had a point – workmen repairing the floor thirty years later found dismembered bodies everywhere, many lying headless and in disarray in tombs that had been either desecrated or hastily dug out entirely without care. According to a publication of the time, *Notices of the Historic Persons Buried in the Chapel of St. Peter ad Vincula in the Tower of London, With an Account of the Discovery of the*

Supposed Remains of Queen Anne Boleyn, the total number of bodies came to a staggering fifteen hundred.

Not all would have been prisoners, as residents of the Tower of London have sometimes chosen to be buried here. But of this total a mere thirty-three could be identified with any certainty, and at Queen Victoria's insistence these were reburied beneath the new floor in a more ordered and respectful manner. Today public services are still held in the church every Sunday, and for more than 150 years a bunch of red roses has been carried anonymously into St Peter's on 19 May, the anniversary of Anne Boleyn's execution.

32. Hampton Court Palace

Richmond upon Thames, KT8

Architecturally speaking the leading figure associated with Hampton Court is Wren, but Thomas Wolsey's lavish riverside domain was conceived as a Renaissance palace – one of the earliest flowerings of the style in England – long before Sir Christopher was summoned to work by William and Mary.

Cardinal Wolsey's ambitions for the palace were immense. Much of what we see today may have come after his time, but his original palace was designed from the start to be larger and more regal than anything possessed by the Crown. Very soon it was, something that almost inevitably contributed to the prelate's dramatic downfall.

No sooner had Henry VIII taken possession of his erstwhile favourite's folly in 1529 than he started work to extend Hampton Court and two hundred years later architects such as Sir John Vanbrugh and William Kent were still hard at it. Many of the most familiar parts of the building are nevertheless Tudor, including the main gateway facing on to the river, the Anne Boleyn Gate behind this, and the profusion of ornate brickwork chimneys that festoon much of the roof.

The influence of the Renaissance is clear to see, however, including features such as the terracotta decoration (for example, the medallions depicting Roman emperors) and Wolsey's taste for geometrically complex ceiling patterns. In retrospect this early adoption of the new continental styles was to be somewhat premature though, and it was to be a century before Inigo Jones and others embraced fully the new classical traditions.

For all that, Hampton Court was by no means a stylistic dead end, and as a visitor it is fascinating to see the development of different architectural fashions as one moves from one part of the palace to another. Hampton Court is also a significant building in that it represents a shift away from devising purely defensive structures to more comfortable and more decorative ones.

The Tower of London may have been a royal palace – legally and technically it still is – but it was conceived and ordered as a fortress first and a residence second. Hampton Court, however, is in part an expression of Tudor confidence and stability; while from outside it still displays the fullest complement of traditional defensive features – including gatehouses, crenellated towers, battlements and, yes, even a moat – these are purely ornamental, and the message they send is unmistakeable. As well as a clear statement of the owner's immense wealth and power, the absence of any real defensive capability serves to underline how, with the Welsh Tudor dynasty accepted and fully bedded in, its sovereign no longer saw any need to hide away in castles or to throw up barriers between himself and his subjects.

33. St James's Palace

Marlborough Road, St James's, SW1

Wolsey's Hampton Court was influential in other ways too. As well as demonstrating the versatility and artistic superiority of brick over stone, it inspired a host of stylistically similar buildings in London as well as further afield. Many of those close to London were built by Henry VIII himself, including the palaces of Whitehall, Bridewell, Placentia and Nonsuch. In all, more than a dozen were completed in the immediate vicinity of the capital – part of a building boom driven by a sudden abundance of land and materials from the dissolution of the monasteries – but of some of them just tiny fragments remain and of others not even this.

St James's Palace, indeed, is the notable exception. Here too the building is by no means entirely Tudor, but many of its most famous and most striking features are, including the octagonal towers of the gatehouse that has closed the view down St James's Street since 1540 (Henry VIII's royal cypher HR can still be seen on this, surmounted by a crown).

Built on the site of an old lepers' hospital, initially as a hunting box for Henry before the destruction by fire of the Palace of Whitehall forced him to move in, it has since provided the backdrop for many significant moments in the history of London and of England. For more than three hundred years it was the primary residence of Britain's kings and queens, and it remains the official residence of the sovereign even though Queen Victoria moved into Buckingham Palace on her accession in 1837.

Every monarch since has followed suit, but foreign ambassadors continue to be accredited to the Court of St James's and it has expanded dramatically over time to accommodate the demands of a growing administration. Attractive buildings now cluster around four inner yards – Ambassadors' Court, Colour Court, Engine Court and Friary Court – and there are more surviving Tudor features in the State Apartments. These include the initials HA, for Henry and Anne (Boleyn), set in a traditional lovers' knot and carved into two fireplaces.

Anne spent the night in the palace after her coronation, and Henry VIII's illegitimate son Henry Fitzroy died here in 1536, a teenager whom the king briefly considered naming as his heir. His daughter Mary signed the surrender of Calais while living at St James's in 1558, and it was from here that her half sister – as Queen Elizabeth – set out to make her celebrated speech ahead of the defeat of the Spanish Armada. Four sovereigns were christened in the palace's Chapel Royal – Charles II, James II, Mary

II and Anne – and while the Prince Regent declined to take up residence here (preferring almost to bankrupt the country by building the short-lived Carlton House at the other end of Pall Mall) four of his eight brothers did so.

Thereafter the popular 'sailor king' William IV was to be the last sovereign actually to live at St James's, but it has continued to be the focus of royal life in London ever since. Queen Victoria married her beloved Albert in the Chapel Royal in 1840 – exactly three hundred years after the Tudors' gatehouse was completed – and important court business is still conducted here on a regular basis in preference to Buckingham Palace.

34. St Helen's

Bishopsgate, City of London, EC3

A rare survivor, London's only nunnery building to escape destruction on the orders of Henry VIII, this church is also a reminder of another important source of Tudor power. Neither royal nor religious, this was the commercial or mercantile drive that developed in London at this time, laying the foundations of the modern City as well as paving the way for the largest empire the world has ever seen.

The original church on the site was dedicated to the mother of Roman Emperor Constantine, although there is no evidence that it was actually built by Constantine (possibly on the site of a Roman or pagan temple) following his conversion to Christianity in the fourth century. The nunnery was founded much later, by the Benedictines at the start of the thirteenth century, the church subsequently gaining a second, parallel nave in order that parishioners and nuns could worship alongside each other but remain separate.

Notable early features include a 'squint' enabling nuns to observe the Mass, but for most visitors the most enjoyable aspect of the church is its profusion of funerary monuments. Many of the best are Tudor and, vastly more numerous than in any other parish church in London, it is these that have earned St Helen's the nickname of 'the Westminster Abbey of the City'.

The survival of so many memorials is something of a mystery. Most obviously it seems extraordinary that such immodest displays of wealth and ego were left untouched by the Reformation, an event that kickstarted an orgy of destruction of religious icons and imagery. It is remarkable too that they escaped the effects of the self-righteous purifying zeal of the early Puritans.

Survived they have, however, and the gain is ours. They include monuments to many City dignitaries including Sir John Crosby (1430–76) whose Bishopsgate mansion was moved brick by brick to Chelsea in 1908 and re-erected (described in the sixteenth century as 'verie large and beautiful and the highest at that time in London's Crosby Hall is still one of the two or three largest private houses in the capital). The founder of the Royal Exchange, Sir Thomas Gresham, was also buried here, in 1579, and in 1609 another wealthy merchant called Sir John Spencer joined them.

Nicknamed 'Rich' Spencer, the latter was Lord Mayor of London, lived on Bishopsgate and was said to be worth £800,000 when he died. Prior to this he had to live with the shame of a daughter eloping with a young peer, and demanding (in a letter that still survives) 'an annuity of £2,200, a like sum for her privy purse, £10,000 for jewels, her debts to be paid, horses, coach, and female attendants'. Elizabeth, the daughter in question, was said to have been smuggled out of Spencer's house in a bread basket, as a consequence of which he refused to pay her more than the sixpence he would expect to pay a baker's boy.

Spencer's memorial is an astonishing piece of Tudor finery, a conspicuously large and magnificent canopied monument set against the south wall of the nave. It consists of a panelled altar tomb on which are recumbent effigies of the deceased and his wife, with Sir John shown wearing armour beneath a long cloak and a ruff. At their feet is the kneeling figure of their daughter, praying, and on either side of the decorated stone tomb two large obelisks with ball finials stand on panelled pedestals. With much in the way of carved enrichment, as well as two inscribed tablets and a host of heraldic decoration, the overwhelming impression is one of indulgence as much as of piety.

The memorial announces that here lies a rich man, a very generous benefactor to the church, and one who is happy for the world to recognize the wealth and splendour of the Tudor City and of the mercantile princes like himself who built it.

35. The Spike

London Bridge, SE1

One of London's most prominent and most conspicuous curiosities – but one that few people seem to notice – the large spike on London Bridge is a fascinating reminder of a particularly grisly part of London's history. Though entirely modern, it marks the place at which, for more than three hundred years, the heads of traitors and others were displayed on spikes at the southern end of the bridge.

This grim but popular practice was not a Tudor invention: the head of William Wallace, that notorious Scottish rebel made famous by Mel Gibson in *Braveheart*, was displayed in this way back in 1305 after being boiled and dipped in pitch to preserve it. But many of the best-known victims were those who fell foul of the Tudor authorities, including Thomas More and Bishop Fisher in 1535 and Thomas Cromwell in 1540. Two years later their decapitated heads were joined by those of Francis Dereham and Thomas Culpeper, the supposed lovers of Catherine Howard. Travelling by barge to her own execution, she would have seen both of them as she passed under the bridge en route to the Tower of London.

In 1598 a German visitor to the city, Paul Hentzner, was able to count more than thirty heads that were still in place. When finally they rotted and fell off, most were just thrown into the river – and the tradition continued until the Restoration.

36. The Charterhouse

Smithfield, EC1

Sir Walter de Manny, as we saw in the previous chapter, gave thirteen acres to the City of London for use as a burial ground during the Black Death. Once the epidemic had receded a small chapel on the site was replaced by a larger Carthusian monastery. Initially a handful of monks were accommodated in what was formally called the House of the Salutation of the Mother of God, but by the Tudor period it had expanded dramatically and was known more simply as the Charterhouse.

Unfortunately neither its size nor status could protect the prior who, in 1535, was among a group of clerics sent by Thomas Cromwell to the Tower of London for 'treacherously machinating' and attempting to have Henry VIII removed as Supreme Head of the Church. In May of that year they were hanged, drawn and quartered, the severed arm of one of them being nailed over the main doorway to the Charterhouse. Further executions followed, and nine of the monks died of starvation after being chained to the wall of Newgate Prison.

Within two years the monastery buildings had been surrendered to the king, from whom the complex passed to a succession of rich, noble owners. The buildings were expensively reordered and extended to create a large and comfortable Tudor mansion, and it was soon sufficiently grand to host Queen Elizabeth before her Coronation and later James I. (When Elizabeth returned for another stay, in 1561, the expense of entertaining her and her retinue literally ruined the owner who was forced into rural retirement.)

In the early seventeenth century the property, decidedly out of fashion, was acquired by Thomas Sutton, conceivably 'the richest commoner in England', who established it as a school for forty-four poor boys with a hospital for eighty poor gentlemen. The school, still known as Charterhouse, eventually relocated to Surrey (in 1872) but the pensioners remained in London, although much of the site – which was badly bombed in 1941 – was ceded to Bart's Hospital Medical School.

Sutton's Hospital (as it is also known) is essentially now an old people's home, and is occasionally open to the public. Behind a large entrance gate on Charterhouse Square, Tudor brick combines with medieval stonework in a way that at this distance seems entirely harmonious, and despite a history of demolition and the change of use it is still possible to see the way in which the original monastic development was remodelled into the home of a nobleman.

For the residents – known as brothers, many of whom even now could at a stretch still be classed under the original descriptions of 'decrepit Captaynes either at Sea or Land' or 'Souldiers maymed or ympotent' – the old Charterhouse continues to provide a wonderful refuge from the modern world. Like the monks before them each resident has a private cell overlooking the central court, and is promised 'a full library and a full stomach, and the peace and quiet in which to enjoy them both'.

37. Golden Hinde

St Mary Overie Dock, Southwark, SE1

Thought to be 'the tideway where ships are moored' as described in *Domesday*, this modest inlet to the east of Tower Bridge is home to Sir Francis Drake's ship, the *Golden Hinde* – a craft that set sail in 1577 with a small fleet of five others in the hope of rounding South America via the Strait of Magellan, thereby avoiding the dangerous waters off Cape Horn.

The voyage was a resounding success, and with permission to loot any Spanish merchants along the way the crew – or rather that half who survived the journey – returned to find themselves heroes. They were also impossibly rich, with some accounts suggesting that even the cabin boy's share of the bounty was sufficient to make him the equivalent of a millionaire in today's terms, while Queen Elizabeth's portion enabled her to clear all her debts.

The *Golden Hinde* that reposes in Southwark is in fact only a replica, as Drake's original survived for more than one hundred years as a popular public attraction at Deptford but was then broken up when finally it began to rot. Its replacement was built in Devon in 1973 using traditional methods and is entirely operational. Since then it has covered in excess of 150,000 miles, including one complete circumnavigation of the globe (1979–80), which is more than Drake managed in his vessel.

What impresses one most now is the size, or rather lack of it. Just seventy-five feet long at the waterline, and barely more than twenty feet wide, it seems incredible that something this size (it is a faithful replica) could so effectively have harried the Spaniards. In so doing it pointed the way to Britain becoming the pre-eminent maritime power, and through this for London to find itself at the heart of an authentically global empire.

38. Staple Inn

High Holborn, WC1

The best and largest piece of half-timbering in London, the range of buildings known as Staple Inn dates from 1585. Though much restored, its regular gables and ornate fenestration continue to provide the modern visitor with a wonderful impression of London's late sixteenth-century streetscape.

As the name and location perhaps suggest, it was formerly one of the Inns of Chancery, the ancient legal enclaves, which once numerous are now reduced to four: Lincoln's and Gray's Inn; and Middle and Inner Temple. This particular one was founded in 1378, taking its name from the building's original function as a weighing place and warehouse for wool, and an important meeting place for merchants practising valuable trade. By 1529, however, Staple Inn had been absorbed into the much larger Gray's Inn, with the buildings behind the spectacular façade eventually redeveloped as shops and offices.

With different owners over the years, and a multiplicity of tenants, it has been altered less sympathetically than it might have been, and restored more often than one might wish. Staple Inn was also severely damaged by enemy action in 1944, when a V-1 'doodlebug' crashed to the ground nearby, and required a near-total rebuild behind the façade, which was not completed until the mid-1950s.

Happily it still pitches and leans slightly drunkenly, but viewed from the street it perhaps looks a little too starched and ironed. This, and its somewhat rackety history, has led some to dismiss what is left as a pastiche. But the alternative view is this: that for its size it is as near as London has to a genuine piece of sixteenth-century London, and as such it is a wonderfully evocative reminder of what whole streets must once have looked like before the Great Fire and other calamities swept them away for ever.

Chapter 6

STUART LONDON

An age of dramatic upheaval and multiple reversals of fortune, the story of Stuart London begins with the foiling of the Gunpowder Plot to kill one king, encompasses the judicial murder of another and the triumphant return to the throne of a third, before ending with the long drawn-out tragedy of Queen Anne's failure to produce an heir.

The population was traumatized as rarely before by the plague and the Great Fire, but there was jollity too with frost fairs on the frozen Thames and radical changes to the landscape of London, the impact of which can still be seen today. As new architectural styles were imported from the Continent, aristocratic landowners began developing the fields between the twin cities of London and Westminster, changing the face of the capital and driving its continued expansion.

39. Prince Henry's Room

Fleet Street, EC4

Given the rapid change and increasing sophistication that characterized the cities of London and Westminster under the Stuart kings, the gateway to Middle Temple might easily be mistaken for a Tudor building. It is actually Jacobean, a building of the seventeenth century that was constructed around 1610. For many years it served as a tavern – first called the Prince's Arms and then the Fountain – before later becoming a museum of waxworks. As a Great Fire survivor it is also the last remaining timber-framed house in central London.

Its ownership is well documented as it remained in the same family from the 1670s until the start of the twentieth century, but over the years many misleading stories have sprung up to confuse its history. Before its restoration by London County Council in 1900, for example, a plaque on the front mistakenly referred to it as a former 'palace of Henry VIII and Cardinal Wolsey'. It has also been described as the 'council chamber' for the Duchy of Cornwall, apparently because a richly moulded plaster ceiling on the first floor bears the three-feathered badge of the Prince of Wales.

In fact it was neither, although the same geometric ceiling is an unusually spectacular piece of work to find in a tavern. A complex pattern of interlocking shapes with ornate foliage decorations and the initials P.H., the quality of its execution makes it one of the finest examples of its kind in the country and it is easy to see how a royal connection might have been inferred. There is another explanation for the unusually rich ceiling decorations, however, which is that they were almost certainly a means of celebrating the fact that James I's son, Prince Henry (1594–1612) became Prince of Wales in the same year that the gateway was rebuilt. Unfortunately he died young, of typhoid fever, leaving his brother to succeed to the throne as Charles I.

40. The Queen's House

Greenwich Park, SE10

If stylistically Prince Henry's Room is the last of the old order, the Queen's House in Greenwich Park is a most emphatic early blast of the new. Required in 1616 to create a new home in a royal park for the bride of James I, celebrated architect Inigo Jones seized the opportunity to introduce the rigour and form of classical architecture to England. Thereafter, and until the Gothic revival some two hundred years later, London barely looked back.

The building is sometimes said to have been an apology to Anne of Denmark after James swore at her for accidentally shooting one of his dogs; but dead at twenty-nine she did not live long enough to see it finished. Instead the property passed to her daughter-in-law, Henrietta Maria of France, Jones completing the work in the newly fashionable Palladian style that he was later to describe as 'solid … masculine and unaffected'.

Today it forms the centre of the most outstanding architectural set piece in London, and is one of the finest anywhere in the world. Seen from the Isle of Dogs – framed by Wren's Royal Naval Hospital, its symmetry wonderfully counterpointed by the Royal Observatory built off-centre behind it – the view of the stark white block is incomparable. Amidst the filth and smoke and blackened brick of seventeenth-century London it must have had the surprise value of a spaceship landing from Mars.

Drawing on classically derived concepts of mathematical proportion and harmony, the building with its clean lines and well-ordered fenestration heralded an entirely new age of architecture at a time when the cosily dark form of Tudor brickwork still predominated. The contrast between the two conflicting styles may be best appreciated walking along Marlborough Road – with St James's Palace on one side, and the pretty, diminutive pastel-shaded

94

Queen's Chapel (also by Jones) on the other – but it was here that the revolution really began, and for this reason alone it remains a crucially important building.

The Queen's House didn't just look extraordinary either, it *was* extraordinary. A sophisticated H-shape straddling the road from London to Kent, for years the traffic actually passed through it along a bridge connecting the two halves, an aspect of its design that is hard fully to appreciate now that the busy road (the modern A2) runs a few hundred yards to the south.

Queen Henrietta Maria called it her 'house of delights', but not everyone enjoyed the new style and when the Parliamentarians commandeered the building Her Majesty's treasures were sold off and scattered. The Queen's House was thereafter demoted to a kind of lying-in chapel for the Roundheads' upper echelons, which was a dignified but rather sad thing for such a glorious and important piece of work.

Henrietta Maria was able to recover much of her property at the Restoration and, in due course, the Queen's House passed to the wives of Charles II and James II and then to a succession of minor royals. Slowly it fell into disuse as a residence, but recognizing the quality and importance of the building Mary II took steps to ensure that it retained its view of the river, hence the separated blocks of Wren's buildings. Later still it passed to the Royal Naval Hospital and then to the Royal Hospital School, at which point it was extended with two new wings and colonnades to celebrate Nelson's victory at Trafalgar. Today it forms part of the National Maritime Museum, albeit separate from the main building.

41. York Watergate

Embankment, WC2

For literally centuries the road linking the cities of London and Westminster was lined with the magnificent riverside palaces of the richest and most powerful subjects in the land. The earliest reference to these dates back to 1237, when the Bishop of Norwich was reported to be repairing his private quay, with the grandest of them – John of Gaunt's Savoy Palace – being burned out during the Peasants' Revolt in 1381. More remarkably, perhaps, the final chapter was completed only as recently as 1874, when the last to survive, the Duke of Northumberland's immense house overlooking Trafalgar Square, was finally torn down.

The large stone Percy Lion that stood on top of Northumberland House can still be seen at Syon Park (across the river from Kew Gardens), but otherwise the only relic of these great ducal and episcopal palaces is this elegant archway dating back to the 1620s. At a time when the Thames was the most hygienic, comfortable and convenient way for an aristocrat to travel through London, the gateway would have formed the ceremonial entrance to York House.

Originally belonging to the bishops of Norwich, it was granted to the archbishops of York in 1556 (hence the name) and eventually passed into the hands of George Villiers. As the 1st Duke of Buckingham, Villiers was a courtier who was showered with so many gifts from Charles I that he is said still to be the most honoured subject in England's history.

Villiers was stabbed to death by a disgruntled army officer in 1628, and York House was confiscated along with many other aristocratic properties following the Civil War. At the Restoration the 2nd Duke (also called George Villiers) was able to recover it – more than seven acres of buildings and land between the river and the Strand – but, never as keen on it as his father, he sold it to developers in 1672. They cleared the house and gardens to make way for George Street, Villiers Street and Buckingham Street (for a while there was even an 'Of Alley', thereby commemorating every element of the former owner's name and title) but happily the watergate survived.

42. The Piazza

Covent Garden, WC2

One of Britain's most successful pieces of urban regeneration, the conversion of an old fruit and vegetable market into a popular retail and culinary destination is a much longer story than it might at first appear.

The rebirth of Covent Garden was kickstarted in the 1970s, and with the obvious exception of St Paul's church on the western side the buildings seem to all intents and purposes to be Victorian. In fact the Piazza – another creation of Inigo Jones – was laid out as early as 1630, and as such is arguably the first example in London of organized town planning around a proper modern town square.

The initiative was the 4th Earl of Bedford's who, observing a gradual westward migration of the rich from the filthy and crowded walled city, decided to develop some land he owned on the former convent garden of St Peter's (i.e. Westminster) Abbey. His ancestors had acquired the site at the Dissolution, and under some pressure from the Crown the Earl of Bedford commissioned Inigo Jones to design a church and three terraces around a central square. The area was intended from the start to be exclusive, but Jones was famously extravagant with his costs, which explains the (possibly apocryphal) request from the client for the church to take the simple form of a barn. At this, the architect is supposed to have replied that he would build 'the finest barn in England'.

The church we see today is indeed simple, but also an extremely bold Tuscan design. Jones drew his inspiration for the square from the Continent too, hence the Italian name *piazza*, and decided to include covered arcades at ground-floor level. These were the first in England, with terraced townhouses built above shop premises to form an attractive, self-contained urban community.

It was an imaginative and unusual concept, but a somewhat risky endeavour that quickly failed. The westward migration of the newly wealthy proved unstoppable – then as now those who could afford to headed for

Westminster and beyond – and before long hawkers and market traders were erecting illegal stalls in an area that very quickly lost its tone.

In 1670 the earl's descendant – eventually to be the 1st Duke of Bedford – petitioned Charles II for a charter to hold a market on the site and, as they say, the rest is history. For the next three hundred years the market thrived, the neoclassical buildings we see today being largely of the 1830s and the dukes of Bedford retaining their freeholds until the early twentieth century (the 11th Duke, after selling up, put the profits into Russian investments that were promptly wiped out by the 1917 Bolshevik Revolution).

By the 1960s traffic congestion had rendered continued use of the old market impractical, and in 1974 it moved to a new site in Vauxhall. The buildings were retained, however, and are an object lesson in restoration and renewal. It is to be hoped that – when the time comes – the rescue of Smithfield Market will be equally successful.

43. The Execution of Charles I

Banqueting House, Whitehall, SW1

The surviving portion of the old Palace of Whitehall, the Banqueting House – another Inigo Jones design, with a magnificent painted ceiling by Rubens – is perhaps best known as the scene of the murder (or execution, opinions vary) of Charles I. Stepping out of a raised ground-floor window onto the scaffold on 30 January 1649, the doomed sovereign famously wore an extra shirt to avoid being seen to shiver – and astonishingly, after more than 350 years, the identity of his executioner has still not been revealed.

A modern information board outside records the event, and on the opposite side of Whitehall the clock above Horse Guards has a painted black mark by the '2' to mark the time of the king's death. For all the horror and tragedy of the day, however, the best memorial to Charles is not here at all but a few hundred yards away, in Trafalgar Square. At the foot of Nelson's Column a mounted statue of His Majesty gazes down on Whitehall, past the place of his execution and all the way to Parliament.

The work of the French sculptor Hubert Le Sueur in 1638, the statue was ordered to be sold for scrap by a vengeful House of Commons after the Civil War. Instead it was rescued and, after being concealed for many years beneath a yard in Holborn, it was eventually returned to the Crown following the Restoration. Commissioning an elaborate new plinth of Portland stone, Charles II had it erected on the very spot from which all distances from London were measured and still are today. In so doing he returned his father quite literally to the centre of London and, it can be said, to the very heart of English life.

44. St James's Square

Westminster, SW1

For more than three hundred years an aristocratic enclave for those seeking proximity to the seat of royal power, the area of St James's was largely the creation of Henry Jermyn. As the 1st Earl of St Albans his loyalty to the king (and a close friendship with Charles II's mother) was rewarded in 1662 with a generous grant of forty-five acres adjacent to St James's Palace.

Jermyn's intention was always to aim high, and St James's Square was from the start conceived as the centrepiece of London's most expensive and exclusive residential area or *faubourg*. While none survives today – the oldest building in the square is No. 4, which was rebuilt for the 1st Duke of Kent after a fire in the 1720s* – the original houses were to be large and conspicuously magnificent, and as such they proved

---

* Now home to the Naval & Military Club, and as such the oldest clubhouse in London, this is the only house in St James's Square still to retain its garden and mews.

irresistible to those courtiers and nobles who could afford the leases.

By the time that No. 4 was being rebuilt the square was already home to a further six dukes and at least as many earls. A decade later George III was born in a house on the east side, and later still the house facing it was to be the childhood home of the future Queen Elizabeth the Queen Mother, the last Empress of India.

Inevitably, in the years since the Second World War the square has become largely (but not entirely) non-residential, but unlike the majority of central London's other squares it has managed to retain its early elegance and atmosphere. The buildings are mostly Georgian or later, but the work of such architectural luminaries as Edward Shepherd, Matthew Brettingham, James 'Athenian' Stuart and Sir John Soane means that the square still gives a fine impression of what Lord St Albans intended.

45. Pudding Lane

City of London, EC3

Besides a small commemorative plaque on an otherwise undistinguished office building there is nothing much to see in Pudding Lane. Nor is there anything of interest about the place besides the fact that it was the origin of the blaze that in September 1666 consumed 13,200 dwellings, nearly 90 churches (including St Paul's Cathedral) 44 livery halls, and innumerable workshops and other commercial premises.

The calamity that we now know as the Great Fire of London began in a baker's shop, which in itself is unsurprising, and it spread like the proverbial wild fire, which is also not that surprising given a strong autumn wind and a city made largely of wood. What is remarkable, however, is how few people died in the Great Fire, although it is almost certainly not true (despite the frequency with which this is reported) that as many people have died jumping from the Monument as fell to the flames.

Six people are known to have committed suicide by jumping off the top of the latter before 1842 (after which a barrier was erected to prevent any more) and the death toll from the Great Fire is traditionally put somewhere between five and nine. But the reality is that many deaths would have gone unrecorded – particularly among the lower classes – and it is also likely that many bodies were effectively vaporized by the ferocity and duration of the blaze.

The upside to this was that the scale of the destruction offered a rare chance to redesign the old walled city from the ground up, to create whole streets, squares and vistas on an entirely new and more rational plan – as, for example, one sees in cities such as Paris, Berlin and New York. Plans to do precisely this were drawn up within literally days of the fire dying down, and shown to the king. But nothing of the sort came to pass, as such a scheme was considered impractical in a place as densely populated and commercially important as London. Instead today we live with the curious but delightful results of a more random and piecemeal approach to redevelopment. Replacement buildings sprang up, and quickly too, and there were new regulations to prevent a similar catastrophe happening in the future; but the rebuilt streets continued to follow the old medieval pattern, and the City of London remained constrained, as it still is now, within the outline of its ancient Roman wall. It is one of many things that makes the Square Mile such a magical place to wander, and long may it remain.

46. The George Inn

Borough High Street, SE1

London's last surviving galleried coaching inn looks older than it is, and indeed the present building (rebuilt in 1676) stands on a site where inns have stood since medieval times.

This being the road to Kent the obvious association is with Chaucer, although his pilgrims set off for Canterbury from the Tabard, which actually stood almost next door until it was demolished in late Victorian times. Shakespeare is a more likely candidate, however, as the Globe theatre is quite close (his plays are still performed here in the summer). And Charles Dickens knew the George too: he mentions it in *Little Dorrit,* and his own father was locked up in the local Marshalsea Prison after falling more than £40 in debt.

Once there were many such buildings in London, and a surprising number survived until the late nineteenth century. Besides the aforementioned Tabard, the Green Dragon off Bishopsgate Within only closed around 1870, the seventeenth-century Oxford Arms in Warwick Lane was pulled down a few years later, and the Old Bell in

Holborn was still trading into the 1890s. Of the three, the Oxford Arms is perhaps the saddest loss, a genuine London landmark the demolition of which caused an outcry and led to the formation of the pioneering Society for the Protection of Ancient Buildings.

Back across the river in Southwark the Queen's Head survived until 1895, but then became a goods depot once railways began to supplant horse-drawn coaches. The George Inn might very well have suffered a similar fate – indeed a further two of its galleries were pulled down to make way for the railway in 1899 – but it is now owned by the National Trust. This and its Grade I listing – nationally only eight working pubs have been accorded a similar level of protection – should mean that its future is secure.

47. Frost Fair

River Thames

During the big freeze of 1963 it was theoretically possible to walk from one bank of the Thames to the other without getting wet, but only for a very short while and anyone wishing to try it had to travel upriver as far as Kingston.

In centuries past, such a treat was far from unusual in London, although the tendency for the river to freeze over depended as much on the design of some of the old bridges as on the temperature of the water. Most obviously, less sophisticated engineering required more numerous piers to support shorter spans, and these worked to slow the flow of the river thereby allowing large areas of ice to form and coalesce.

On such occasions Londoners, keen to grasp an opportunity for fun and profit, flocked down to the river to enjoy the kind of impromptu entertainments we now call frost fairs. Such things have a long history in the capital, with archery and other pursuits taking place on the river in the 1560s and many thousands of citizens enjoying themselves at the last of them before the demolition of the medieval London Bridge in 1831 put a stop to the entertainments.

The most extraordinary, however, took place during the reign of Charles II, when a 'mighty frost' from December 1683 until the following February led what one contemporary observer described as a 'winter wonderland' to spring up in the heart of London. The thickness of ice – put at between ten and eighteen inches – and the length of time for which it remained frozen, was unprecedented. The year is now thought to be the coldest ever recorded in London, and very quickly a whole street of temporary shops and stalls was erected, running from Temple Gardens to the opposite bank.

Even the king and his family travelled down to the river to witness the spectacle for themselves – as in earlier years Henry VIII and Elizabeth I had done – and with some daring a fire was lit on the ice that was large enough to roast an ox. Another visitor, the diarist John Evelyn, cheerfully describes the many other activities on offer, including 'sleds, sliding with skeetes, a bull-baiting, horse and coach races, puppet plays and interludes'. The result of all this, he says, not to mention some rather lewder sports, 'seemed to be a bacchanalian triumph, or carnival on the water'. The thaw, when it came, was rapid. By 6 February it was possible to navigate from one bank to the other in a small rowing boat, and the following morning all the ice had broken up and dispersed.

Other fairs followed – in all there are thought to have been fifteen – but most lasted much less than a week. The ice for the last big one (in 1814) was sufficiently thick for an elephant to walk across the river at Blackfriars, but within four days there was nothing left. Two hundred years later Londoners are still waiting for the next fair.

48. The Tomb of Queen Anne

Westminster Abbey, SW1

The Stuart dynasty began with a new sovereign being summoned from across the border in Scotland, and at its conclusion required another to be found from even further afield. George I was not only foreign-born but probably would have preferred to remain in Hanover, and certainly he left instructions that his body was to be returned there when eventually he died.

The failure of the Stuart line comes down to Queen Anne. It is true she had more than forty relatives who were closer to her than George and so might have continued the line, but the 1701 Act of Settlement prevented (and at the time of writing still prevents) a Roman Catholic from succeeding to the throne.

She and George of Denmark had many children too, of course, Anne falling pregnant at least seventeen times between 1684 and 1700, but none survived. This alone makes her grave in Westminster Abbey an especially sombre place, a dozen miscarriages and stillbirths (and not a single child surviving until its twelfth birthday) combining in one life both immense personal tragedy and, ultimately, a dynastic disaster.

Considered kind but dim (much like her devoted husband) Anne was happily married but unhealthy for almost her entire life. As a young woman she suffered from a debilitating eye condition known as defluxion, and afterwards missed her own sister's wedding as she had smallpox. At other times she is thought to have suffered from a variety of illnesses, including porphyria, lupus, diabetes and gout. Although it should perhaps be said that, aside from gout, many of the other diagnoses are ones made in retrospect rather than by her personal physicians.

It is known that she was tremendously overweight, and one of her nicknames – 'Brandy Nan' – speaks volumes. Contemporary portraits of her invariably show a slim and attractive woman, but at her coronation she was so lame that six Yeomen of the Guard had to carry her into Westminster Abbey under a canopy – she was only thirty-seven – and so grossly overweight that the ceremonial golden spurs could not be affixed to her ankles. At her death in August 1714 her coffin – which is said to have been almost square – had to be carried by a phalanx of pallbearers chosen more for strength and stamina than style or status.

Not yet fifty, Anne's passing was by any measure a sad end to a colourful dynasty – and to a life that no one but the most virulent republican would have wished on her.

Chapter 7

GEORGIAN LONDON

The first city anywhere in the world to reach a population of a million, the fact that so much of Georgian London has survived intact – public buildings as well as private ones, and in places such as Belgravia and Bloomsbury entire, unspoilt streets and squares – explains why it is perhaps the earliest version of the capital that the visitor can properly visualize and understand.

Immense fortunes were established during this period (some of which survive today), for example by the owners of outlying fields who cleverly transformed them into highly prized streets and squares. As England asserted its dominance over much of the world, so London did over the rest of the country; although home to just 10 per cent of the population, London controlled as much as 75 per cent of the country's trade.

49. Geffrye Museum

Kingsland Road, Hackney, E2

This exceptionally handsome and well-proportioned set of livery company almshouses was laid out in 1714, meaning that it could conceivably be London's oldest Georgian building.

For the last hundred years it has housed a museum of domestic interiors, the rich and varied collections arranged in a series of room sets to convey an impression of how lifestyles and living have changed in London since around 1600. Before being acquired for this purpose by London County Council in 1914, the almshouses were owned and run by the Worshipful Company of Ironmongers, one of the 'Great Twelve' livery companies that have overseen mercantile and trade activities in the City of London since medieval times.

Many such organizations still survive, of course, including the Ironmongers who as the 'Ferroners' were active in the capital as early as 1300.* Then as now their function

---

* At the time of writing there are 108 livery companies, including several new ones – such as the Firefighters, Master Mariners and Information Technologists, which were established in the twentieth century.

was essentially twofold, namely to protect the commercial interests of members and to fund various charitable and educational enterprises. The provision of almshouses such as these formed a tradition of long standing, and indeed the Ironmongers and other livery companies continue to endow and administer sheltered accommodation projects in London and elsewhere.

Forming three sides of a square, the Geffrye takes its name from Sir Robert Geffrye (1613–1703), a successful East India merchant and former Lord Mayor of London. It was his generous bequest that paid for the new building, originally to house fourteen pensioners most of whom were widows of liverymen. A few other livery-funded almshouses have survived in the capital, but none is quite as delightful as this one with its gardens and simple architectural formality. Its use as a museum of interior decoration is also highly apposite, as this area of Hackney was for many years an important centre of furniture and cabinet making.

50. Chiswick House

Hogarth Lane, Chiswick, W4

An austere but spectacular expression of the classical ideal, having adopted the form of a Tuscan villa Chiswick

House is perhaps London's most surprising country house. 'Too small to live in, too big to hang on a watch', the 3rd Earl of Burlington's creation remains one of the most intriguing and elegant private homes in London. The enigmatic description of it by one of his many aristocratic visitors was perfectly phrased, although in reality the exceptionally handsome eighteenth-century house was never intended to be even remotely practical.

Burlington at no point planned to live in it, although he would not have foreseen the bruising conversion of his Palladian idyll into a hospital in the 1890s and then, even more bizarrely, into a fire station in the 1940s. (Nor, one suspects, would he have guessed that only the most strenuous lobbying by the Georgian Group would prevent the local council from pulling down what is now recognized as a highly important Grade I listed architectural gem, and one of the country's most outstanding country house designs.)

Richard Boyle, 3rd Earl of Burlington and 4th Earl of Cork (1694–1753) had inherited his titles and fortune as a very young boy, and from the age of ten devoted his life to the appreciation and understanding of the arts, in a fashion that was quintessentially Georgian. To contemporaries he was even known as 'the Apollo of the Arts' and, 250 years later, the association is just as strong with his London residence, Burlington House on Piccadilly, home to the Royal Academy and other learned societies.

Where most men of his class and inclinations made one Grand Tour of Europe, Lord Burlington made several; and while many a gentleman amateur liked to dabble in architecture Burlington actually practised it professionally. In this his expertise and ambition meant he was instrumental in the acceptance in England of Palladian principles and, simultaneously, he managed sufficiently to impress George Frideric Handel that the king's *Kapellmeister* dedicated two operas to his host while staying as his guest.

Survivors of Burlington's inspired neoclassicism can be seen at Westminster School, York Assembly Rooms and a number of English country houses; but, with so many of his works since altered or destroyed, Chiswick House is by far the most interesting and the most visited.

Built not to live in but to display Burlington's collections of furniture, books and art, it was also somewhere that he could entertain and – even more than this – a personal act of *homage* to the Italian architect Andrea Palladio. An authentic piece of Renaissance Italy magically translated to what was then London's rural fringe, its setting in one of the first English landscape gardens (created by William Kent, who also worked on the interiors) caused a sensation in the 1730s, and even now a million visitors a year flock to see its spectacular plasterwork, Rysbrack sculptures and lavishly carved fire surrounds.

After the death of its creator it passed to the dukes of Devonshire, the 4th of whom had married Burlington's daughter. With so many other country houses, including their seat at Chatsworth, Bolton Abbey in Yorkshire and Lismore Castle in Ireland, the dukes made little use of it, however, although Georgiana Spencer, the socially prominent wife of the 5th Duke, entertained fashionable and political figures in what she termed her 'earthly paradise'.

Georgiana's friend, the leading Whig statesman Charles James Fox, died here in 1806, as did George Canning (in the very same room) after serving a mere 119 days as prime minister. The 6th Duke briefly introduced an elephant, giraffes, elks, emus and kangaroos to the park, but by his time the house was in marked decline and after narrowly escaping demolition it was rented out in the 1850s.

For more than thirty years it was a private mental hospital before being taken over by Middlesex County Council in the 1920s. As custodians they were far from perfect, but in 1956 the old Ministry of Works began to put the old house back together again. A decade after that, The Beatles arrived to shoot a couple of promotional films in the conservatory.

More recently archaeologists have located the remains of an old Jacobean house in the grounds – the building Lord Burlington chose to live in, and which was torn down after his death – and a £12 million restoration has done much to return William Kent's idyllic landscape and the park's decorative temples and follies to their former pristine glory.

51. Shepherd Market

Mayfair, W1

The Georgians, besides their self-evident talent for designing and building beautiful country houses, were also exceptionally skilled town planners, and as London expanded a number of landowners followed the example of Lord St Albans in St James's by building smart new suburbs to the west of the city's historic centre.

The best of these – like the Bedford Estate's 'little towne' of Bloomsbury (see below) – were elegant, self-contained communities, although of course there was at this time no attempt to make them socially mixed in the manner we have come to expect. For obvious reasons, landlords and property speculators at this time built primarily for the wealthy; the poor and middling classes were typically left to subdivide and occupy the rundown properties that the rich left behind as they abandoned the filth and squalor of the City and migrated west.

These new houses for the great and good had to be serviced, however, and behind the great streets and squares a variety of markets and tradesmen's stalls sprang up to supply the goods needed to fuel and feed the houses of nobles and others. With the West End no longer primarily residential most have disappeared, so that Shepherd Market is now the only one to have survived in anything like its original form. That said, and as is only to be expected given its location, it is these days a good deal smarter and more exclusive than it would have been back in 1735.

It is built on the site of the old May Fair, the annual event from which the area takes its name and which was eventually banned when a rowdy and lewd element threatened to get out of hand. The architect-builder Edward Shepherd, spotting an opportunity, created a little warren of shops and taverns running off Piccadilly, somewhere that soon thronged with servants exchanging gossip about their employers and collecting the daily provisions.

A quick visit reveals that none of the buildings is original, but the network of narrow streets and passages means it still has the atmosphere of the eighteenth century. Many of the great houses have similarly disappeared or been converted into offices and hotels, but here it is still possible to appreciate (and applaud) the way in which little markets such as this one would have provided such an important amenity to the kitchens, sculleries and stable yards of London's rich.

52. The London Jamme Masjid

Brick Lane, Spitalfields, E1

The United States of America is so often described as a melting pot of many different races, a nation of immigrants, but much the same can be said for London and for hundreds of years it has been true. The evidence is everywhere, but perhaps no single building better describes the way in which successive waves of immigration have changed the face of London and its ethnic make-up than Brick Lane's Great Mosque.

The building itself dates back to 1743, when as 'La Neuve Eglise' it was established by Huguenot refugees who settled in this part of east London after escaping persecution by the French Catholic authorities. The community eventually moved on, many of them to Wandsworth where the borough's coat of arms still contains three rows of blue teardrops, or *gouttes azure*, representing the tears and suffering of the dispossessed French. In 1809 their church in east London, no longer needed, was taken over by the Wesleyans, then by a short-lived organization seeking to convert Jews to Christianity, and later by the Methodists.

The next big change came towards the end of the nine-teenth century – when east London's Jewish community declined to convert to Christianity, 59 Brick Lane was reconsecrated as the *Machzikei Hadas*, or Great Synagogue. In this guise it was to serve another large and important influx of refugees, this time of escapees from Tsarist pogroms and then from Nazi Germany.

Once again the change of use was to be temporary, and as these latest arrivals moved into more prosperous areas of north London their place was taken by yet another new wave of immigrants. This time they came from the Indian subcontinent, chiefly people from Bangladesh who came in search of work and found it in what was still then a thriving local textiles industry.

By the mid-1970s the Bangladeshi community was numerous, well-established and flourishing. Needing a place to worship they acquired the old disused synagogue in 1976, and remodelled it to suit their own purposes. As a Grade II listed building it has retained its neat, symmetrical Georgian appearance, and regularly accom-modating up to three thousand worshippers it continues to serve this part of London as it has done for more than 270 years.

53. Spencer House

St James's Place, SW1

We saw in the previous chapter how, once Henry Jermyn began to develop his precious acres around St James's Palace, this latest addition to the London streetscape was very rapidly colonized by nobles and others seeking to be close to the court. Inevitably some parts of his lordship's development were more sought after than others, with St James's Square, for example, attracting the most aristocratic buyers, and Arlington Street attracting so many politicians that it was soon nicknamed 'Minister Street'.

Away from the prestigious central square the most favoured addresses were those overlooking Green Park, a location that quickly gained a reputation as 'one of the most beautiful situations in Europe, for health, convenience and beauty'. Here, it was said of one house that the prospective owner could take full advantage of an address that at the front stood 'in the midst of the hurry and splendour of the town' while 'the back is in the quiet simplicity of the country'.

Such a description would certainly have applied to Spencer House, as well as several other equally grand private palaces overlooking Green Park. In the quiet cul-de-sac that is St James's Place, its entrance front presents a relatively modest and dignified face to its neighbours, but at the rear, viewed across a private terraced garden and the park, Spencer House displays all the glory, exuberance and extravagant decoration of an elaborate eighteenth-century showpiece and of a family approaching its peak in terms of wealth and power.

The house was completed in 1766 for the landowner and courtier the 1st Earl Spencer, having been designed for him by John Vardy, William Kent's pupil and a fellow Palladian. Even now, his rusticated ground floor and immense portico make the garden front one of the great sights of Green Park, while the interiors (by other hands, including Henry Holland and James Stuart) are if anything even more elaborate.

Unfortunately it was arguably too grand for the Spencers. The family was eventually to return to prominence (in the person of Diana, Princess of Wales), but within a hundred years of its completion a great London palace was possibly stretching their resources. Accordingly, after the furniture and art had been removed to their Althorp estate in Northamptonshire, Spencer House was let to a variety of tenants and the Spencers retreated to the country.

For a while it provided a London base for the 9th Duke of Marlborough and his wife, the former Consuelo

Vanderbilt, and later the (now defunct) Ladies' Army & Navy Club. Then, having emerged relatively unscathed from the war, it was converted into offices and used as such from 1948–85. Managing somehow to survive this as well, it was then rescued and beautifully restored by the 4th Baron Rothschild and, still in his care, it is opened to the public most Sundays.

With Charles Barry's positively ducal Bridgewater House on the one side, and on the other 22 Arlington Street by William Kent, Spencer House is by no means a unique survivor in this part of London. But it is arguably still the prettiest and most delightful – and the easiest to visit – and as such provides a wonderful reminder of a time when London was so compact that it really was possible to live with one foot in it and the other outside.

54. Bedford Square

Bloomsbury, WC1

London in the eighteenth century was a large, vibrant and rich world city, but not everyone liked what they saw. In 1725 Daniel Defoe declared unequivocally that its streets, squares and new buildings were 'the like of which no city, no town, nay no place in the world can shew', but other writers were less certain. Mayfair's Grosvenor Square was dismissed by an American visitor as 'a collection of whims ... without anything like order or beauty', while one of the founders of the Royal Academy lamented that the rest of the West End had been 'left to the mercy of ignorant and capricious persons'.

The problem, according to architect John Gwynn, was a lack of any 'pretension to magnificence or grandeur' – meaning essentially that there was no real attempt at planning – but in Bloomsbury things were about to change. In 1775 much of the area belonged to the Russell family, dukes of Bedford, and in laying out what is now London's most immaculate, regular and complete Georgian square the widow of the 4th Duke (acting as regent during her son's minority) created a superb example of Georgian urbanism at its best.

What John Evelyn described with some accuracy as 'a little towne', Bloomsbury grew from this. Its well-ordered streets and squares (together with mews to serve them) were also to provide the blueprint for other London landlords, most of them aristocrats seeking to monetize their once valueless fields and meadows, which suddenly were within reach of the rapidly expanding capital. Indeed the richest and most aristocratic of them, the Grosvenor family – viscounts, earls, marquesses and later dukes of Westminster – even went so far as to poach Thomas Cubitt from under the noses of the

Bedfords when it came to developing their London estate in the 1820s.

Working for the Grosvenors in Belgravia, Cubitt built houses for the most fashionable and wealthiest elite. But here in Bloomsbury his terraces were intended very much for the aspirant middle classes, although to modern eyes the houses seem – and are – large, conspicuously grand and, yes, noble. Sadly, few are now residential, and of those not many have escaped being divided into flats. But they have survived, which is important, and in sufficient quantities to retain the largely unified feel that Bloomsbury's creators sought to achieve.

That they have done so is something to celebrate, for very few areas of London have fared so well. The surprise, however, is how much of the destruction that has taken place needs to be laid at the door of the university and museum authorities rather than the German Luftwaffe. While now these authorities quite naturally defend their surroundings, and seem on the whole to be good custodians, the truth is that as recently as the 1970s the very cultural institutions that give Bloomsbury its special character were the ones fighting to destroy its Georgian splendour and to replace this with hideous, faceless, brutal blocks.

55. Parish Watchhouse

Giltspur Street, EC1

As crime-ridden and corrupt as it was elegant, progressive and well ordered, the Georgian period was also to become something of a golden age for capital punishment, when Londoners could be executed for the theft of as little as five shillings (twenty-five pence).

With some justification cynics have suggested that the sudden escalation in the number of capital crimes – at their peak more than two hundred individual offences carried the death penalty – was simply an exercise in avoiding the heavy cost of incarcerating convicts for long periods. More cynical, however, is the idea that such a steady flow of cadavers suited the burgeoning medical profession, whose interest in anatomy was increasing rapidly. Its members were keener than ever to secure bodies for dissection – at this time the boundaries of medical science were being pushed back at an impressive rate – but until the 1832 Anatomy Act only the bodies of criminals were permitted to be used in this way.

Unsurprisingly the latter – or more particularly their families – would often go to great lengths to prevent further indignities being heaped on the hanged and beheaded in this way, which only added to the problem that there were rarely enough bodies to go round and demand invariably exceeded supply. A new class of more entrepreneurial criminals quickly sprang up, who made it their business to supply the medics by digging up fresh corpses from London's churchyards. Few of these so-called resurrection men went so far as Edinburgh's Burke and Hare – who ensured a ready supply by murdering their victims first – but their activities naturally panicked the population.

Incredibly the crime was not considered particularly serious – typically it was a common law misdemeanour rather than a felony – and in 1747 two men were fined just a shilling each with a few months in Newgate after the body of a child disappeared from a grave in Whitechapel. It is also difficult to assess just how widespread was the practice, as it was in the interests of neither buyer nor seller to come clean about their involvement in the gruesome trade.

That said, some indication of the scale can be measured by the presence of watchhouses such as the one in Giltspur Street near Smithfield. Built and manned so that the authorities could keep an eye on the graves of the recently buried, this particular one was erected in 1791 in the churchyard of St Sepulchre and therefore predates the Anatomy Act by some years.

The proximity to Bart's Hospital means that those buried here were conceivably at extra risk of being exhumed, but watchhouses of this sort were once common across London. (Not all were as robust as this one, however, and at Bunhill Fields one watchman's hut – with him inside it – was bundled over the wall by a gang of thieves.) They were still being built right up to the time that the Anatomy Bill was being debated – Lambeth Parish Watchhouse was completed in 1825 – and some survived into the 1930s although by this time the ineffectiveness of the lowly paid watchmen meant that their duties had long ago been taken over by the Metropolitan Police.

56. Somerset House

Strand, WC2

Completed in the mid-sixteenth century, the first Somerset House was one of the immense Strand palaces of the rich and powerful (see previous chapter). Lord Protector Somerset's Renaissance demesne – the first in England to adopt this influential style – was built using materials salvaged during the destruction of the priory of St John Clerkenwell and from an old charnel house attached to St Paul's.

The first of its kind to be built in London, its replacement that we see today was conceived in the 1770s as a vast complex to house government offices, a function it continued to fulfil for the next two hundred years. During the late eighteenth and early nineteenth centuries the terraces by William Chambers also provided a home for various learned societies – including the Royal Society, the Royal Academy of Arts and the Society of Antiquaries – but this was at a time when these were emphatically inward-looking institutions so that the entire building was effectively completely off-limits to the public.

Today it seems quite extraordinary that such a glorious and exciting space could have barred its doors against visitors for so long, and that until very recently the huge open courtyard, which is now such a draw, offered no more amenity than car parking for civil servants. However, shockingly, this is no more or less than the truth. For a while the Royal Navy occupied the part of the building that overlooks the Thames, appropriately enough at a time before embanking when the river literally washed up against the terrace below. But for much of its history one of central London's largest and most splendid buildings was used for nothing more glamorous than accommodating the Stamp Office, the General Register of Births, Deaths and Marriages, and thousands of men and women working for the Inland Revenue.

Its rebirth in the 1990s was thus long overdue, and today its renovation and remodelling as an exhibition space – for the Courtauld Gallery and the Gilbert Collection of gold, silver and objets d'art – must be counted among the most significant moves in the cultural rebirth of the capital. With room for contemplation, study and world-class exhibitions as well as for more light-hearted entertainments – in the summer children play in the fountains, at Christmas the courtyard is transformed into an ice rink – Somerset House is now such a fixture on the London scene that at times one struggles to recall a time when, for most of us, it was no more than words on government circulars.

57. Cockpit Steps

Birdcage Walk, SW1

Until it was outlawed in England in 1835, cockfighting enjoyed a long run as a spectator sport, with a history going back as much as six thousand years and a particularly strong following in London from the sixteenth to eighteenth centuries.

This small cut-through from Old Queen Street, a twisting run of stone steps now Grade II listed, commemorates the presence near here until around 1816 of the Royal Cockpit, one of the more famous of the many venues for cockfighting in Georgian London. While often used to characterize the colour and atmosphere of life among the lower orders, such activities in reality had huge appeal for all classes, one visitor to this particular pit describing 'a collection of peers and pickpockets, grooms and gentlemen, *bon vivants* and bullies'.

As its location and name perhaps suggest, the upper classes were by no means strangers to the sport: many entered their own gamecocks into the vicious bouts, and many more came to spectate and to bet on the outcome. Cockpit owners took a cut as well as charging admission, and with some authorities on the sport suggesting that entry to the Royal Cockpit could cost as much as five shillings (twenty-five pence) it seems reasonable to suppose that any rougher, working element would have been forced to find its entertainment elsewhere. The sport was nevertheless brutal and awful, the birds – their wings trimmed and wattles removed – fighting to the death under the watchful eyes of a 'teller' and two 'setters', and a noisy, feverish, heavy-betting crowd.

58. The First Gas Works

Great Peter Street, SW1

The first use of gas for domestic lighting took place in the West Country in the 1790s, and in 1807 part of Pall Mall was illuminated by gas to celebrate the birthday of the Prince of Wales. Both were merely demonstrations, however, and it took until 1812 before Georgian London fully embraced the technology and established its first commercial gas works.

The Gas Light and Coke Company was incorporated by Royal Charter in Great Peter Street by F.A. Winsor, the German inventor and entrepreneur who had been responsible for the Pall Mall show a few years earlier. Almost certainly the first public gas works anywhere in the world, the company was authorized to provide lighting to the cities of London and Westminster using coal gas, and rapidly expanded with works in Whitechapel and Poplar, and at the Royal Mint (by the Tower of London).

Over the course of the next hundred years or so the company absorbed around a dozen rival concerns in London and elsewhere, and survived intact until it was nationalized in 1949, by which time its customers stretched from north London out to the Thames estuary.

Today the company is recognized as the direct ancestor of British Gas plc and Centrica. Besides a plaque marking its foundation in Westminster, a number of historical artefacts have survived from the early days. These include an authentic Georgian gasholder at Sands End, Fulham (the world's oldest); the Beckton Gas Works in east London, which was named after company chairman Simon Adams Beck; and a tug, MV *Barking*, the sole survivor of a near forty-strong fleet of colliers and other company vessels.

59. Brixton Windmill

Windmill Gardens, SW2

Scores of street, place and pub names incorporating the word windmill – and one very famous West End theatre – are all that remain of most of the windmills that once served the capital. That seven have survived is perhaps more remarkable than the number that have disappeared, and inevitably these are on the whole to be found far closer to the perimeter of London than to its centre.

Of the seven this is by far the most central, and dating from 1816 it would have enjoyed an open outlook for its first few decades as this area comprised mostly market gardens and pastureland until well into the mid-nineteenth century. Built by a local family, the Ashbys, it ceased operating in the 1860s by which time the expansion of south London had effectively cut off its source of power. Conversion to steam nearly half a century later (and then gas) gave it a new lease of life, but in the 1950s the 140-year-old structure was acquired by the London County Council who returned it to its original condition.

Sadly it has been vandalized on a number of occasions, and the local borough council has struggled to find new uses for a building that, while charming, represents a potentially huge drain on resources. In 2008 a campaign was launched to raise £2 million for its continued restoration, and now plans are in place to start producing flour again in time for the Georgian mill's 200th anniversary.

60. Royal Opera Arcade

Charles II Street, SW1

London's first covered shopping arcade, this was designed by John Nash and G.S. Repton during their remodelling in 1816–18 of the old Italian Opera House. At the time this was the largest theatre in the country – today it is Her Majesty's – and one of London's smartest with the audience in even the cheapest seats required to wear evening dress.

Nash and Repton's modifications included the addition of colonnades on three sides of the theatre, with a narrow arcade on the fourth providing a cut-through from Charles II Street to Pall Mall. With its run of elegant Regency shop fronts to one side the Royal Opera Arcade was quickly deemed a success and the idea – already popular on the Continent – proved highly influential.

Other similar arcades began to appear elsewhere in the West End, including Burlington, Princes and Piccadilly arcades, and in Bloomsbury an alternative was tried in Thomas Cubitt's delightful bow-fronted Woburn Buildings (now Woburn Walk), which was completed in 1822.

No longer as fashionable as once it was, Royal Opera Arcade has in truth lost out to some of its imitators, in particular Burlington Arcade with its uniformed beadles and charmingly arcane regulations. But its significance is not to be underestimated for in its day it represented a radical departure for shop owners as a class who, prior to this time, had attempted very little if anything in the way of display or product promotion.

Instead, when provisioning was typically done by servants rather than their mistresses, and seen as a daily chore rather than a leisure activity, shop windows tended to be small, the choice of goods limited, and the merchandise typically stacked up behind the counter. For literally centuries it had been this way, but now the Royal Opera Arcade found itself in the vanguard of a genuine retail revolution, a tentative first step towards the idea of consumption as something pleasurable rather than necessary. More than this it was the first example in London of what we would now call shopping as a destination, a phenomenon we now take for granted with the West End known the world over for the quality and incredible variety that it offers to even the most discerning shopaholic.

Chapter 8

VICTORIAN LONDON

From a city of just over a million at the start of her reign to one of nearly 4.5 million at her death, in a single lifetime Victoria's London was utterly transformed. The changes came as a consequence not just of this unprecedented growth but also because of the coming of the railways and the impact at every level of society of administering and maintaining the largest empire the world had ever seen. At once a place of great wealth and unimaginable squalor, just as Georgian London bequeathed the most civilized ideal of urban living so it was the Victorians who designed and built much of the infrastructure on which Londoners still depend.

61. Kensal Green Cemetery

Harrow Road, W10

Emblematic of the Victorians' obsession with death, but also of their unwavering commitment to progress and technology, this wonderful north-west London landmark pioneered a new fashion for funerals at a time when the burial grounds and ancient churchyards of the historic city could no longer cope with the demands being placed upon them.

For decades the rich had been insulated from problems of overcrowding because spaces for interments inside church buildings could usually be found for those with money and influence. But outside conditions were appalling, with churchyards literally overflowing. Coffins of the long dead were frequently being dug up, broken up and burned, and the bodies of the more recently interred were often so badly buried that there were reports of limbs breaking the surface and concerns about 'fatal miasmas' affecting those living nearby.

The answer was clearly to move the dead away from the centre of the metropolis – 'to places where they would be less prejudicial to the health of the inhabitants' – and following a Parliamentary Act of 1830 new commercial entities sprang up to create many hundreds of acres of stylish suburban cemeteries.

At Kensal Green the first of these, the General Cemetery Company (GCC), had from the start the highest ideals. On more than fifty acres many hundreds of trees were planted, the entire area carefully landscaped, and chapels built in the most fashionable Greek Revival styles – Doric was selected for Anglican mourners, Ionic for the non-conformists – behind a vast Doric entrance. Plans for a watergate were abandoned – allowing coffins to arrive via the Grand Union Canal – but the latest technologies were adopted, including a hydraulic lift to take the deceased from the main chapel down into the catacombs below.

With space for ten thousand bodies in the catacombs alone there was, in short, to be nothing second rate about these suburban burials. Amidst a welter of publicity the GCC saw its share price more than double as the great and good – led by two of George III's offspring – embraced the new fashion. Soon everyone who could afford to was seeking to reserve a plot in the aesthetically pleasing surroundings of Kensal Green, its appeal best expressed by G.K. Chesterton in his poem 'The Rolling English Road' in which he wrote: 'There is good news yet to hear and fine things to be seen, before we go to Paradise by way of Kensal Green.'

Others followed, but Kensal Green set the pace. The celebrated landscape gardener J.C. Loudon gave it a tacit seal of approval when he was buried here in 1843, and Princess Sophia and HRH the Duke of Sussex were soon joined by writers such as William Thackeray and Anthony Trollope, the composer Michael Balfe and several Brunels including Sir Marc, his wife, and their son Isambard Kingdom. Today, town dwellers in particular take for granted the idea of large, municipal cemeteries, but to the Victorians it was a radical concept born of necessity, but one whose time had come.

62. Thames Tunnel

Wapping–Rotherhithe, SE16

At Rotherhithe is another connection with that great dynasty of civil engineers, the Thames Tunnel, completed in 1843 by Marc Brunel and his son and still in daily use more than 170 years later.

The first modern tunnel under a river, its gestation was long and tortuous. The initial idea to run horse-drawn carriages under the Thames had caused a genuine media storm when the project was first mooted in 1818 – Brunel Snr was already becoming something of a celebrity – but as problem piled on problem even supporters began to talk of Brunel's 'great bore'.

He had earlier patented a 'tunnelling shield', apparently inspired by the common shipworm *Teredo navalis* during a period in prison for debt, designed to protect the workforce as they burrowed into the ground. Supporting the newly excavated tunnel while it was being lined with brick, its twelve massive cast iron sections would then inch forwards on hydraulic jacks as the work progressed.

The idea was good but its execution less so, and it took several years and another visionary engineer to perfect it: Sir James Greathead, one of the unsung heroes of the creation of the London Underground system. Brunel, meanwhile, was to be dogged by disaster. His mechanical digger failed for want of an engine powerful enough to turn the blades, and the first fatality (of ten) came within a fortnight when one of the labourers fell down a shaft. A few months later the Thames broke in, flooding a tunnel that had advanced barely more than ten feet, and following a gas explosion and complaints about the fetid, dank air down below, many of those engaged in digging were soon reporting to be suffering from boils, strange lesions, nausea and diarrhoea.

When a key engineer collapsed and died from overwork less than a year into the project, Marc's diminutive son Isambard came on board to assist, but he too was soon expressing concern at some of the debris that the diggers were finding (suggesting they were working horribly close to the bed of the river). In pretty short order the men went on strike; the tunnel, which leaked constantly, flooded again – killing two more – and Brunel Snr suffered a paralysing stroke. After making a partial recovery he decided that a party was in order to cheer the workers and some forty VIPs, and a banquet was organized for nearly two hundred, with music from the Coldstream Guards.

As a public relations exercise this worked a treat, but a few weeks later the tunnel was flooded again, this time filling up so quickly that Brunel Jnr was forced up to the surface by the torrent before emerging at what is now Wapping tube station (he was fortunate, whereas two other men died). The Brunels were also broke, and with the tunnel only half completed the government stepped in so that they could finish the job.

Eventually they did so, and on 27 January 1843 the young Queen Victoria was present to open the tunnel, to make Marc Brunel a knight, and to see the first of an estimated fifty thousand Londoners who filed through the tunnel that first day. Alas the taxpayers' largesse had extended only so far. With no funds left to build the spiral ramps needed to admit carriages, the tunnel became a footway only, and once again the public's early enthusiasm rapidly died away.

Almost immediately colonized by muggers and prostitutes, and briefly even considered for conversion to a sewer, thereafter the Thames Tunnel really only came into its own when it was taken over by London Underground for its East London Line. This ran until 2007, the oldest part of the network, and today it forms part of the London Overground network, with the Brunels' unusual horseshoe-shaped tunnel still largely intact.

63. Palace of Westminster

Westminster Bridge Road, SW1

Augustus Welby Northmore Pugin may have characterized his most famous creation as 'all Grecian, sir. Tudor details on a Classic body' but the fact remains that what he devised while working with Charles Barry is still arguably the definitive Victorian building, not just in London but in the entire country.

A new home for the House of Commons and the House of Lords (as well as literally hundreds of offices and committee rooms, for the debating chambers are surprisingly small and account for a tiny proportion of the building) was urgently required after the devastating fire of 1834. This had started in a furnace below the Lords' chamber – carelessly overstocked – and destroyed a complex of buildings that had been at the heart of English government for some three hundred years.

A competition to design a new Palace of Westminster attracted an impressive ninety-seven entries, with many leading names throwing their hats into the ring with a variety of different styles. Still to be knighted, Barry won the competition. But more confident working in the classical milieu than in the increasingly popular Gothic, he formed a working partnership with the young Pugin, who was well versed in Gothic having illustrated a number of his father's books in the style.

Working on the project from 1840 until 1852 the partnership proved to be perfect: the older man providing the form and bones of the building and the technical expertise; and Pugin – destined to die, insane, at the age of just forty – taking responsibility for the overall feel of the building and its almost overwhelming decoration.

There is no doubt that without Barry's expertise and diplomacy there would have been no building, but today it is Pugin's work that arouses the most comment and which, one suspects, endears the building to those who work in it and visit it. With a taste for the picturesque, the Bloomsbury-born Pugin covered every surface with a richness and variety of detail that has seldom been bettered.

Much of this was in a largely self-invented Gothic Revival style and, applied to seemingly every surface, vertical and horizontal – as well as doors and windows, furniture, fireplaces, bookcases and more – the effort nearly killed its creator. Claiming never to have 'worked so hard in my life for Mr Barry' Pugin came close to collapse while insisting on taking personal responsibility for everything – tiled floors, panelled walls, stained glass, wallpapers, clocks, even the inkwells.

Almost his last act before slipping into madness was to hand Barry his design for what is officially now the Elizabeth Tower but known everywhere as 'Big Ben' (in actual fact this is the nickname of the largest bell that hangs inside). Barry was eventually knighted for his work here, but it is probably fair to say that in the Palace of Westminster it is Pugin who now has the most astonishing memorial.

64. Albertopolis

Exhibition Road, SW7

The ceremonial entrance to Kensington Gardens, known as Coalbrookdale Gates, is one of the few remaining relics of the Great Exhibition of 1851. Technically ingenious – each sixty-foot gate was cast in a single piece at Ironbridge in Shropshire – they were made to stand at the entrance to the north transept of the Crystal Palace and were moved here after the Great Exhibition had closed.

Today it seems quite incredible that something as huge and celebrated as the 1851 extravaganza could have almost entirely disappeared, but in fact in the area of South Kensington nicknamed 'Albertopolis' there are still plenty of reminders. As the name suggests, and as with the Crystal Palace itself, much of the impetus came from the Prince Consort personally, a far-sighted and highly energetic individual who fastened on the idea of using the profits from some six million visitors – equivalent to Britain's entire population at the time – to create something of lasting worth and value.

In particular, Albert wished to set aside a large site lying to the south of Hyde Park Gate and Kensington Gore, and to create an area for the arts, sciences and education generally, with museums, concert and lecture halls, libraries and so forth. Like the man himself the idea was not universally popular (indeed the name 'Albertopolis' was at first satirical), but with a profit of more than £186,000 to dispose of he had the resources to aim high and to achieve something quite remarkable (also, it has to be said, to achieve something uniquely Victorian in its commitment to progress and technology).

Today a substantial part of his legacy survives, and it encompasses several institutions of world renown, including Imperial College London, the Natural History and Victoria and Albert museums, the Royal Albert Hall, the Royal Geographical Society, and the Royal Colleges of Art and of Music. A number of other colleges have amalgamated or been absorbed into larger institutions, and of the great Imperial Institute nothing now survives except the nearly three-hundred-foot bell tower designed by T.E. Collcutt, architect of the Savoy Hotel. Even so, gazing down from his memorial, Albert would have good reason to smile.

Could the same have been achieved today? Almost certainly not, and for so many different reasons. But in a sense this doesn't matter, for Albert's inheritance is still there to be enjoyed and draw profit from; his institutions are generally in fine shape, and after well over 150 years that really is something to celebrate.

65. Crystal Palace Steps

Sydenham Hill, SE19

Joseph Paxton's great glass conservatory was of course removed to a grassy hill in south-east London at the conclusion of the Great Exhibition, although much like the Dome a century and a half later it struggled for a while to find a purpose and the first company to take it on went spectacularly bust.

For nearly eighty years it formed the centrepiece of a magical two-hundred-acre park, containing gardens and a boating lake, a zoo, sporting facilities and an extraordinary array of twenty-nine life-size models of dinosaurs. Created in brick and stucco by sculptor Benjamin Waterhouse Hawkins, and seeming quite wacky now, the latter nevertheless represented the state of man's knowledge at the time, a key adviser to the project being anatomy professor Richard Owen who had first coined the term 'dinosaur', meaning terrible lizard.

The dinosaurs have survived, and are in good shape following their recent restoration. But of the mighty Crystal Palace itself nothing now remains but a few steps up to the plinth on which it stood until all was consumed by fire in November 1936. Perhaps the best that can be said is that standing on the steps it is still just about possible to get an impression of its size: a building taller than Nelson's Column, it covered nineteen acres, required more than ninety thousand square feet of specially made glass panels and more than five thousand workers to complete – and which, let us not pretend, no one but the Victorians would even have contemplated building, never mind moving it to Sydenham.

66. Royal Arsenal

Woolwich, SE18

What was eventually to become the largest armaments complex in the world can trace its history back to a seventeenth-century ordnance-storage depot, but it was in the 1850s – during the preparations for the Crimean War – that what was in effect London's military suburb expanded to become one of the real engines of Victorian imperial might.

In the 1670s the original depot had covered just over thirty acres, but with the addition of a Royal Laboratory (for experimentation with new forms of explosives and ammunition) and a Royal Brass Foundry (for producing

guns) the site expanded very much in step with Britain's colonial possessions. Eventually it was to cover more than fifteen hundred acres and at its peak employed an incredible eighty thousand men and women.

With the Royal Navy's historic Woolwich Dockyard nearby, the Royal Military Academy and the barracks of the Royal Regiment of Artillery, security in this area was always paramount. In the late eighteenth century convict labour was brought in to construct a wall more than two-and-a-half miles long and in places as much as twenty feet high, a structure reinforced and extended by the Victorians, and until quite recently the whole site was still shown on the *London A–Z* as no more than a blank space.

Much of it survives today and is easy to access. Great stretches of the wall still surround the site, with some of the best Georgian and Victorian buildings converted to museum, commercial and residential space in the years since the last military personnel left in 1994. Because of this it is still possible to get an excellent idea of how vast this place once was: with a 1,060-foot façade, for example, the barracks were for decades the widest building in London. That Woolwich was just one of three Royal Armaments factories close to the capital (the other two being at Waltham Abbey and Enfield) also reinforces just how much technology and raw firepower was needed to acquire and retain an empire the size of Britain's.

67. The First Drinking Fountain

Holborn Viaduct, EC1

Around the corner from the Giltspur watchhouse (see previous chapter) is London's oldest public drinking fountain, installed in 1859 on the boundary wall of the churchyard of St Sepulchre-Without-Newgate.

For many centuries the capital's water was heavily polluted with domestic sewage and commercial waste, and for London's poor the safest alternative was often beer, a relatively sterile beverage. To counteract the obvious effects of this the Metropolitan Free Drinking Fountain Association was established by Samuel Gurney MP, a philanthropically minded Quaker and a scion of the eponymous banking dynasty.

In the wake of the 1854 cholera epidemic, Gurney sensibly favoured siting his new fountains as close as possible to pubs, in this case the Viaduct Tavern. It was declared open on 21 April 1859 and was soon being used by up to seven thousand people per day, although the charity never attracted sufficient donations despite broadening its remit by renaming itself the Metropolitan Drinking Fountain and Cattle Trough Association.

With the resources of the family bank behind him (Gurney's merged with Barclays Bank in 1896) Gurney decided to underwrite its activities himself, and more than eighty fountains and troughs were installed during his lifetime. Two more elaborate ones survive at Finsbury Square and New Bridge Street, but this one – the first, and with its cups on chains – is historically more significant.

68. Paddington Station

Praed Street, W2

Railways have long been emblematic of the Victorians' drive for technological progress, and among the great London termini it is perhaps Paddington that has the strongest claim on the visitor's attention.

Architecturally it may lack the profile and distinction of St Pancras, with its soaring Gothic verticality and stylish Champagne Bar, and it has none of the romance of Waterloo, under whose clock lovers and others have arranged to meet for as long as anyone can remember. But unlike the other great railway sheds that still ring central London it was to play a crucially important role in the development of an entirely new breed of railway, one that was to transform London and be copied literally the world over.

The station buildings we see today were designed by the great pioneering engineer Isambard Kingdom Brunel in the 1850s, although by this time the site had already been in use by the Great Western Railway for more than twenty years. In 1863, however, an entirely new service began running trains under the ground rather than over it and from Paddington into the City of London. This, the tentative beginnings of the Tube network, was the brainchild not of an engineer but of the official Solicitor to the City authorities, Charles Pearson (1794–1862).

As early as 1845 Pearson had described what he called an 'Arcade Railway' running along the bed of the old Fleet River from Farringdon to a new railway terminus at King's Cross. Pearson envisaged 250,000 passengers per day riding 'a majestic eight-track covered way, thoroughly lighted and ventilated' and hoped to alleviate London's already terrible traffic congestion by providing 'frequent, punctual and cheap intercommunication between the City and suburbs'.

In the event, Paddington was selected rather than King's Cross, and Pearson died just months before his scheme reached fruition. His plan to run trains through shallow tunnels just a few feet below street level was adopted, however, not least because advances in tunnelling technology meant that the first true deep-level 'tubes' were still nearly thirty years away.

Not everyone thought that the first underground railway anywhere in the world was such a good idea. One vociferous preacher famously warned that burrowing under London in this way would disturb the Devil, and the satirical weekly magazine *Punch* dismissed the whole thing as a 'sewer railway'. But its success seemed assured even so, and following an inaugural run on 10 January 1863, thirty-eight thousand commuters per day were soon crowding into its steam-pulled wooden carriages.

The new service was called the Metropolitan Railway, and such was its influence around the world that several imitators, most famously the Paris Métro, are still named after it. More than 150 years later it is also extraordinary to think that the trains of the Metropolitan, Circle, District and Hammersmith & City lines running into Brunel's great terminus still use the stations and tunnels envisaged by Charles Pearson, something that helps explain the relative abundance of light and air when compared to the Central, Jubilee and Northern lines.

69. Trinity Buoy Lighthouse

Trinity Buoy Wharf, E14

Yet more evidence of the Victorian commitment to new technology, London's only lighthouse – who knew it even had one? – was built in 1864, a few years after the ancient Corporation of Trinity House was given jurisdiction over all English lighthouses and navigation markers.

As the name suggests, the wharf was for many years where the corporation stored buoys used on the Thames, as well as a maintenance depot for its lightships (one of which is still moored here, having been converted into a recording studio). The lighthouse – the second on the site – was designed by Sir James Douglass, the engineer responsible for the famous Eddystone light, and was used not to aid navigation but as a laboratory and test-facility for lights later employed around the coast, and to train new keepers.

Among those who used the facilities here was Michael Faraday, a key figure in world science whose wide-ranging interests included the construction and design of lighthouses. Born at the Elephant and Castle, almost entirely self-taught and never quite considered a gentleman – for a while he even served as Sir Humphry Davy's valet – his success was an early example of a meritocracy at work, but as such by no means typical of London at this time.

70. Leadenhall Market

Gracechurch Street, EC2

A gem of glass and cast iron, the present building was completed in 1881 although a market had existed here since the 1370s. At that time 'foreigners' – which is to say anyone but those resident in the walled city – were permitted to sell poultry and later dairy and other produce to the people of London. The market expanded rapidly, particularly after the Great Fire, by which time it was selling not just provisions but also agricultural byproducts such as leather and wool.

In the 1990s the cobbled pathways and ornate ironwork of the Grade II listed structure were painstakingly restored, together with the green, maroon and cream-painted market buildings designed by Sir Horace Jones (architect of the City's two other historic markets, Smithfield and Billingsgate). With its diverse range of bars and restaurants, and many specialist and luxury retailers, the market is now a popular meeting place for City workers and visitors, a happy coincidence as the site is now known to have been occupied by the Roman Forum, the social and indeed geographical centre of Londinium.

71. Jack the Ripper's First Murder

Durward Street, E1

Capturing the public's imagination like no other serial killer before or since – which is slightly odd as he was by no means London's most prolific – Jack's popularity might be easier to explain were it possible to visit the locations of his gruesome mutilations and find something close in appearance to what was there in 1888.

The reality, however, is that the endless cycle of building and rebuilding denies modern-day visitors the chance to wallow in the sinister and slightly dangerous atmosphere of nineteenth-century Whitechapel. Some unspoilt corners remain, and at one of them a ghastly murder was even perpetrated at the same time the Ripper was active. But no serious authority now attributes the death of Martha Tabram in Gunthorpe Street to the mysterious Jack, so instead amateur Ripperologists looking for the mean tenements where he sought his prey mostly find only office blocks and in one case a multi-storey car park.

In Durward Street a litter-strewn yard in front of the old Board School is now perhaps the closest one can get to the Ripper, this being where the body of a forty-one-year-old prostitute was found in the early hours of 31 August 1888. There isn't much to see today, but there wasn't back then either, although the discovery of the mutilated corpse of Mary Ann Nichols was sufficient to spread panic at the idea that an anonymous killer was at large in the streets of Whitechapel.

The discovery of another body less than a fortnight later, and then two more a couple of weeks after that, understandably set panic levels soaring. By the time a fifth was discovered literally everyone in east London knew about the Ripper and his modus operandi. Today, our fascination, one suspects, has less to do with the number of women he killed and the brutality he showed than with the fact that he was never caught or identified and – unlike almost every other serial killer on record – seems to have stopped his killing spree as suddenly and inexplicably as he began it.

72. Public Lavatory

Foley Street, W1

Public loos are by no means a Victorian invention: the Romans introduced them to Londinium, and Henry III reportedly spent £11 on building such a facility near to London Bridge. The oldest in London are certainly Victorian, however, well-timed to take advantage of Sir Joseph Bazalgette's extensive network of magnificent new sewers and a fine example of the nineteenth-century approach to urban planning and infrastructure.

In Star Yard WC2 there is a rare decorated cast-iron pavement urinal, painted green, Grade II listed and out of commission since the mid-1980s. This is decidedly more of a Parisian *pissoir* than one might expect to find in London, however, most of its contemporaries being buried beneath the pavement in a somewhat more decorous fashion.

But these too are now largely derelict, although some surprising new uses have been found for a number of them. A few years ago plans were made to turn one (in Kennington) into an art gallery; in Crystal Palace an architect has remodelled another into a stylish subterranean apartment, complete with a tiny private garden; and here in Fitzrovia a third built in 1890 has been reborn as a smartly minimalist café. Long vacant, now occupied, and located beneath the pavement near the Crown & Sceptre pub, its meticulously cleaned and polished urinals have been cleverly converted into intimate breakfast booths as part of the imaginative £100,000 project.

Chapter 9

EDWARDIAN AND PRE-WAR LONDON

In many ways not much changed from its Victorian predecessor, Edwardian London nevertheless espoused a new kind of progress as well as an obsession with modernity and the benefits of new technologies such as the motor car. Where the railway age had accelerated the growth of London, the Underground now began to unify the sprawling metropolis. Once developers had done no more than acknowledge rigid class structures by building only for the rich and aspiring classes; now utopian planners began to experiment with the first genuinely mixed communities. Similarly, where architecturally the choice for decades had been limited – essentially between classical and Gothic – now old conventions were being discarded as a proliferation of new styles and new ideas came to the fore.

73. The Black Friar

Queen Victoria Street, EC4

From the great nineteenth-century battle between classical and Gothic Revival architects emerged a vigorous new form known as the Arts and Crafts Movement, and on a cramped site on a noisy river, road and rail junction on the edge of the City this tiny pub provides the perfect introduction to it.

Narrowly escaping demolition in the 1960s (following a protest campaign led by Sir John Betjeman) the pub dates back to the late nineteenth century, although the highly original wedge-shaped design we see today is emphatically Edwardian. The exterior by Henry Poole and others dates from 1903 and in its distinctive mosaic decoration with the figure of the friar himself over the corner entrance references the old Blackfriars Monastery that once stood here.

The ground-floor interior was completed two years later by H. Fuller

Clark, and is a cheerful, unrestrained riot of multicoloured marble with more mosaics as well as decorative copper, brass and bronze work and elaborate fire baskets. Around the walls busy reliefs depict jolly monks singing hymns, collecting fish and eels – perhaps it is a Friday – and boiling eggs. The quasi-religious iconography and the strange slogans incised into the stonework – *Finery is Foolery – Haste is Slow – Industry is All – A Good Thing is Soon Snatched Up* – provide a charming if romanticized link with the past, and it is incredible to reflect that such a place could once seriously have been earmarked for destruction.

74. Hampstead Garden Suburb

NW11

On land given to Eton College by Henry VI this early exercise in utopian suburban planning was the 1906 brainchild of philanthropist (Dame) Henrietta Barnett who conceived what would now be termed a mixed community – 'a green golden scheme' it was called at the time – of rich, poor and intellectuals.

Not everyone she recruited to the cause saw things quite her way – Sir Edwin Lutyens thought her nice but 'proud of being a philistine' – but others, notably Raymond Unwin and Barry Parker who had laid out Letchworth Garden City, found her energy infectious and shared many of her ideals.

Adopting simple, broadly seventeenth-century vernacular styles, which now make the houses in the area among the most sought-after in north-west London, the pair laid out an imaginative pattern of tree-lined streets and cul-de-sacs, with houses grouped together rather than just strung out in rows. Unusually for London the street plan also respected the natural contours of the landscape rather than simply seeking to conceal them beneath monotonous lines of brick and tarmac.

In keeping with the original plan the housing provided is a combination of flats for artisans, villas for the middling sort, and much larger houses for the wealthy. Bespoke accommodation was also provided for old people and working women – a very advanced notion – although perhaps predictably the mix was never quite as integrated as the instigators had hoped. In particular the larger houses, even here in Utopia, mostly occupy the best sites, meaning that the better off residents were then and still are today located mostly to the south where the suburb meets the broad expanse of Hampstead Heath.

75. Russell Square Station

Bernard Street, WC1

One of the outstanding aspects of London's Underground is the way in which it manages to unify a huge, diverse and widely displaced conurbation, and it is extraordinary how even now many Londoners still navigate by visualizing a version of Harry Beck's world-famous map of the Tube when travelling across London by car, bus or even on foot.

The Underground network – the world's first – was never conceived as a single entity, however, and until the 1930s the individual lines were owned and operated by different private companies and run according to different rules.

While it is unlikely that any one of the early movers and shakers entertained serious thoughts about taking over sufficient of their rivals to own and run the entire network, some of the more visionary recognized the benefits of a system that gave the appearance of being unified, and certainly appreciated how a degree of corporate branding could achieve this.

One such was the buccaneering American Charles Tyson Yerkes, who today is recalled mostly for an entirely despicable business model – 'buy up old junk, fix it up a little and unload it upon other fellows' – but who had some pretty advanced ideas for his time. An early stroke of genius had been to employ the architect Leslie Green to design a series of new stations for the several railway companies he owned (and which today we know as the Piccadilly, Bakerloo and Northern lines).

Yerkes wanted to establish a coherent design theme for his new lines and stations, which he told Green needed to be bold, distinctive and, most importantly, 'fully equal to those of the best stations on the [rival] Central London Railway'. Green, just twenty-nine at the time, chose a strong, uniform Arts and Crafts style for this, brilliantly adapting it to suit some fifty or so individual sites and combining it with some of the most advanced engineering and building methods of the Edwardian period.

Like this station, those he built are immediately identifiable, even now, thanks to his use of ox-blood-coloured 'Burmantoft's Faience' for the façades, a traditionally manufactured tin-glazed terracotta block. Behind this were strong, easy-to-assemble, structural steel frames of a type newly arrived from the United States, a combination that proved to be highly cost-effective, cheap and easy to maintain, and instantly recognizable in even the busiest streets without being so outlandish as to offend.

The steel structures also allowed for spacious uninterrupted interiors – perfect for ticket halls – and permitted the space above the stations to be developed and let for office use or accommodation. Yerkes was therefore able very quickly to recover most of his costs, while the fact that so many of Green's stations are still in use today speaks volumes for the quality and integrity of his pioneering and highly intelligent design.

76. Frithville Gardens

W12

A reminder of London's first Olympic Games, this nondescript West London street – once a fashionable Japanese garden – is the sole surviving remnant of the so-called White City that was created for the 1908 Franco-British Exhibition.

Conceived to celebrate the 1904 Entente Cordiale,* the exhibition attracted more than eight million visitors – considerably more than the more famous Great Exhibition of 1851 – but is now all but forgotten. Instead the 140-acre site with its immense water features and gardens and more than forty acres of white stucco pavilions (hence

---

* This refers to a series of agreements that were signed in April 1904 between the United Kingdom and the French Third Republic to settle a number of longstanding colonial and commercial issues.

the name) is lost beneath the Westfield Shopping Centre, housing and what remains of the BBC Television Centre.

In truth it was never intended to be permanent though, and indeed survived far longer than it might have done but for Britain offering to stage the IVth Olympiad when it became apparent that Italy could not afford to do so. The offer was accepted but only late in the day, and with little time to prepare it was decided that the logical thing to do would be to host the Games at White City.

Much like Stratford a century later, this was a place with good transport links and situated sufficiently far from the city centre to avoid London grinding to a halt. A new stadium was required, however, and in record time a new sixty-eight-thousand seater was completed with a running track and swimming pool at a cost of just £60,000. Opened by Edward VII in April 1908 – and remaining in use until the mid-1980s – it is now considered to be the precursor to all modern stadia.

77. Selfridges

Oxford Street, W1

Another American newly arrived in London to extend his fortune, Harry Gordon Selfridge had been a partner in

Chicago's Marshall Field but when he struck out on his own decided to cross the Atlantic, apparently in order to avoid competing with his former colleagues.

There was competition here too, of course, but whereas the likes of William Whiteley and Charles Harrod had begun as small shopkeepers and grown their businesses gradually, Selfridge could afford to think big, and did so. He was backed by Samuel Waring of Waring & Gillow, on condition that his new store did not sell furniture (a condition Selfridges respected until long after W&G had ceased trading); but he had his own resources too, which he threw into the project from the word go.

The store opened in 1909 and the West End had never seen anything like it. Dominating one side of Oxford Street its forceful neoclassical design appears today to be typically Edwardian but was the work of another American, Chicago architect Daniel Burnham. A vast retail palace with dozens of giant Ionic columns, an immense clock above the main entrance and the towering figure of 'The Queen of Time' more than twice life-size, it contrasted strongly with the messy jumble on either side and made a powerful statement of confidence from a magnate who never doubted he would triumph.

Selfridge himself had some strange ideas: his plans to build a mausoleum on the roof had to be abandoned when it was explained that his scheme was so over-the-top that the store beneath would collapse under the weight.

And for a while he was so sure of his idea to have Bond Street Station renamed Selfridges Station that he planned a tunnel from the trains right into the store.

But he was shrewd as well. The first to observe that 'the customer is never wrong' he was the first to fit out the ground floor as a large beauty hall (still the world's largest, it is a move every department store has copied) and paid John Logie Baird to demonstrate his new 'televisor' in the store to would-be customers. Many Londoners saw their first aeroplane here too – thousands queued all night to see Louis Blériot's monoplane go on display after his flight across the Atlantic – and while Selfridge himself came to a sticky end (an extravagant playboy, he was eventually removed from his own board and died poor) the shop still bears his name after more than a hundred years and is still an authentic London landmark.

78. Sicilian Avenue

Bloomsbury Way, WC1

Providing the strongest possible contrast with Selfridges (and yet the two are near contemporaries) Bloomsbury's second exercise in small-scale retail planning – after Woburn Buildings – is the pretty little Sicilian Avenue, which opened in 1905. Linking Southampton Row to Bloomsbury Way, this introduced London to the idea of traffic-free shopping at a time when the capital was becoming increasingly motorized.

Once again the style is classical but there is none of the bombast of Selfridge's great emporium, just a short diagonal cut-through with a short colonnade or screen at either end. The shops and cafés on either side are highly decorative, a mixture of brick and terracotta with turrets and large display windows positioned between columns rising through the first two storeys. The effect has been described as playful – which it is, rather than grand – and although it has taken a century for the Continental habit of outdoor eating and drinking finally to reach this country, it here makes more sense than almost anywhere else in London.

79. Royal Automobile Club

Pall Mall, SW1

The motor car was invented in 1885, London's first multi-storey car park opened in 1901 (in Denman Street, behind Piccadilly Circus) but it was to be almost another half-century before technology finally triumphed and the last horse-drawn cab (a four-wheeled 'growler' working the rank at Victoria Station) was finally nudged into retirement. With hindsight one could say it was never going to be any other way, but the horse had been dominant for literally centuries and, in the early days at least, these new-fangled automobiles had as many enemies as they had friends.

The latter were a largely middle-class lot, the aristocracy being traditionally hippophilic and conservative, and the poor unable to afford an opinion let alone a vehicle of their own. A highly clubbable bunch, these pioneering automobilists soon set about establishing their own base in London. This was to be somewhere to meet others like them, but also a place from where they could campaign on their own behalf and evangelize about the benefits of new technology.

With this in mind the building created for them in 1911 (on the site of the old War Office) was to be a technical tour de force, designed by Charles Mewes and Arthur J. Davis, a leading architectural partnership of the day, a pair adept at combining modern practicality and convenience with a certain classical majesty. Not everyone was happy with the choice, and members of the much older, socially smarter clubs of St James's Street were soon to be complaining about the arrival in Pall Mall of these 'motorious carbarians'.

The building nevertheless was to be technologically hugely advanced, and equipped with the latest luxuries such as a beautiful subterranean swimming pool – still the best in London – its own post office and a rifle range. It was also built on a truly mammoth scale, covering more than an acre and employing a revolutionary new type of internal skeleton with a two-thousand-ton steel matrix supporting a near 230-foot Portland stone façade.

With foundations going down more than sixty feet – revealing several Georgian cesspits and the remains of an actual mammoth – the finished building boasted facilities rarely before seen in England. These included electric and hydraulic ascending rooms or lifts, centralized vacuum-cleaning and heating systems, fireproof floors, air-conditioning, a communications network comprising 120 telephone lines, automatic ice-makers capable of producing five tons in a week, even electric lights similar to those installed at Sandringham for the king – by W.J. Crampton, a member.

Admittedly in clubland the old boys still call it the 'Chauffeurs Arms', a reference to it being by far the least exclusive of its peers. But walking through this cool, elegant and undeniably handsome landmark – and observing how seamlessly its design blends tradition and technology – one wonders whether some of its neighbours aren't simply jealous.

80. The New 'Air-Age' Arrives in London

Tower Bridge, EC3

In a sense the perfect meeting point of old and new in London, the late-Victorian Tower Bridge was designed to complement a medieval fortress but within its twin towers housed some of the most innovative technologies of its age.

Briefly it had a brush with some even more advanced machinery, however, in the summer of 1912 when pilot Frank McClean flew his new Short Brothers seaplane up the Thames towards this world-famous London icon.

McClean had taken off at 6 a.m. from the brothers' new factory at Harty Ferry on the Isle of Sheppey in Kent and, as *Flight* magazine was to report in an edition dated 17 August, on approaching London he 'brought his machine lower down and negotiated the Tower Bridge between the lower and upper spans. The remaining bridges to Westminster he flew underneath, the water being just touched at Blackfriars and Waterloo bridges. He reached Westminster about 8.30 and was taken ashore to Westminster Pier.'

How many people witnessed his feat is not recorded, but it turned McClean into an overnight celebrity. The action was one of a daredevil, but his intention had been deadly serious – namely to demonstrate to the authorities that if a seaplane could land on the Thames then why not on the Nile or elsewhere in the British Empire?

The following year he spent three months negotiating a route to Khartoum by plane, but the Great War put a temporary halt to any further experiments in transcontinental flight. The idea was clearly sound, however, and with others following his example – notably Sir Alan Cobham who flew a frail de Havilland DH-50 from Kent up to Westminster Pier, but via Australia – its day came soon enough. By the 1930s flying boats of Imperial Airways were plying regular routes to Britain's Indian and African colonial possessions and, although a second war with Germany put a stop to that, McClean's hunch had been proved right.

Years later, intriguingly, Tower Bridge was to enjoy another brush with technology, this time with the jet age. In 1968 a young Royal Air Force pilot was placed under arrest after 'buzzing' Parliament in his Hawker Hunter fighter and then flying between the towers of Tower Bridge. Hundreds of Londoners were naturally thrilled by this daringly impromptu celebration of the RAF's fiftieth birthday, but just as naturally the top brass were puce with fury. Having avoided the chilly waters of the Thames, Flight Lieutenant Alan Pollock quickly found himself in very hot water and discharged – but today, surely, he deserves a plaque on this, one of the world's most famous bridges.

81. Admiralty Arch

Trafalgar Square, SW1

Part of Sir Aston Webb's great ceremonial route to Buckingham Palace, and a clever way to link Trafalgar Square to the axis of the Mall, the arch is also a tribute from a son to his mother.

The inscription to this effect is said to be the largest in London – ANNO : DECIMO : EDWARDI : SEPTIMI : REGIS : VICTORIÆ : REGINÆ : CIVES : GRATISSIMI : MDCCCCX (In the tenth year of King Edward VII, to Queen Victoria, from most grateful citizens, 1910) – although by the time it was completed, two years later, Edward too had died and passed the baton to his own son, George V.

Like the spectacular Victoria Memorial at the far end of the Mall it is glimpsed at every royal occasion but otherwise overlooked, and indeed having been used as government offices for years the Grade I listed building has recently been let to developers for conversion to a hotel.

82. Arsenal Stadium

Highbury, N5

London and football have a long history. Fulham FC existed as far back as 1879 – at first an amateur church side, the team had originally been called St Andrews – while in the 1880s Arsenal (then known as Dial Square) recruited its players from workers at the aforementioned Royal Arsenal in Woolwich, hence its nickname – the Gunners.

The first southern team to join the Football League, in 1913 the club crossed the Thames to occupy a ground in Highbury, which it retained until 2006. The lease at the time specified no matches were to be played on holy days, and no liquor was to be sold on the premises as the owners were St John's College of Divinity. In the event both clauses were abandoned within months of the team moving in, and eventually the club was able to buy the ground outright.

To Arsenal fans Highbury was not simply a temple to working-class culture but also, always, the real home of football. That claim gained additional traction following the demolition of the old Wembley Stadium in

2003, and certainly it is the most striking of the London grounds from an architectural standpoint. Admittedly its most famous features might more correctly place it in the next chapter (London Between the Wars), but the truth is that it is impossible to picture the Edwardian pitch without them.

The features in question are the east and west stands, completed in the 1930s in an art deco style and rapidly incorporated into Arsenal's distinctive iconography. Designed by Claude Waterlow Ferrier and William Binnie, and now Grade II listed, both survived the club's relocation to a new ground in 2006. While Wembley's equally revered twin towers were pulled down in the face of many protests, these north London landmarks were preserved and have since been converted into apartments.

Chapter 10

LONDON BETWEEN THE WARS

Britain triumphed over German aggression in 1918, but only at an immense cost. Not just in terms of casualties – although the scale of these is horrifying even now – but also in terms of national prestige and self-confidence. The mighty British Empire was to soldier on for a few decades longer, but the Armistice in a very real sense signalled the end of an era and amidst calls for 'Homes for Heroes' London in peacetime seemed torn between two opposing poles.

On the one hand there were moves to emphasize the strength and solidity of what had gone before, with many public buildings – including most obviously the Bank of England – adopting a stately, imperial style, a resolutely British form harking back to the past glories. But elsewhere there were signs of change, and a willingness to seek inspiration abroad. Cinema and theatre designers mimicked Hollywood with fantastical creations in such unlikely settings as Brixton and Kilburn High Road; other architects embraced the machine age with gleaming Streamline Moderne designs, such as the Hoover Factory on Western Avenue and Bloomsbury's glorious, curvaceous Daimler Hire Garage.

Today, of course, it is hard to assess this brief period in London's long history, not least because no one could know then that they were *between* wars. Certainly the period started out with optimism and a determination to overcome the depredations of a terrible war but, as the 1930s drew to a close and Europe darkened once again, Londoners began to hunker down.

83. Becontree Estate

Barking and Dagenham, RM8

It is unlikely that David Lloyd George personally coined the phrase 'Homes for Heroes', but never one to pass up a useful, vote-catching slogan it was the Welshman who promised to improve the lot of the former conscripts who flooded in from Flanders and elsewhere, broken, disenchanted and visibly undernourished.

Created by London County Council in 1921 Becontree was one of the early attempts at meeting that promise, a building scheme of such staggering proportions that nearly one hundred years later it is still one of the largest public housing schemes in the world (with more than twenty-seven thousand dwellings and a population of one hundred thousand, England has smaller cities).

As much as anything the estate was an exercise in social engineering, and one that had a profound effect on London by providing the blueprint for several later initiatives such as the New Towns of the 1950s and 1960s. These emptied out much of the inner city by encouraging growth around the periphery, a move that is far easier to understand and accomplish now that most adults drive cars but which was quite radical at the time.

Such schemes were always controversial, but had much to recommend them. Entire communities were disrupted and even destroyed, and there was no attempt at Becontree to create a real heart or 'town centre'. But the slum clearances were necessary and long overdue, and while many of the houses on the estate were cheaply built and cold in winter Becontree families had gardens and indoor sanitation, neither of which had been a feature of working-class life in the East End.

84. King George V Dock

North Woolwich, E16

Since that first Roman wharf nearly two thousand years earlier London continued to dominate British trade for centuries: it remained the country's pre-eminent port until well into the 1970s, and the docks themselves were the world's busiest throughout much of the eighteenth and nineteenth centuries.

A sense of their scale can be gauged from the crime figures over this period. It has been estimated, for example, that by the eighteenth century at least £500,000 of goods were being pilfered annually from vessels moored in the Thames, with companies expecting to lose up to a half of each consignment and the authorities acknowledging that one in three dockworkers was stealing or receiving.

At a time when as many as one hundred thousand Londoners were officially considered to be to some degree criminal, the problem was always more acute in the docks and it is no coincidence that Britain's first police force was established here (the Marine Police Force formed in 1798, more than three decades before the regular police were operational). It also explains the immensely high walls surrounding the newer wharves – some of which survive at St Katharine Docks – and why dock companies designed special pocketless uniforms for workers in which goods could not be concealed readily.

Congestion on the river only added to the problem. With as many as sixty thousand ships unloading per year, and the banks lined on each side with a near-continuous wall of wharves, eight thousand vessels at a time could queue for literally weeks before being unloaded. To alleviate the worst of this, and to expand London's capacity, a series of enclosed docks were excavated to the east.

Until the creation of the Port of London Authority in 1908 to administer shipping between the Tower and Tilbury, these docks were built and run privately. They were created on a heroic scale, with the last of them – the King George V, completed in 1921 and now the site of London City Airport – covering some sixty-four acres.

Joining the Royal Albert and Royal Victoria docks, it represented what might be termed the high water mark for London shipping. At a time when Britain was still, famously, the workshop of the world, the Royal Docks accounted for 250 acres of working water stretching more than ten miles east of Tower Bridge. Together they enabled the Port of London to handle an incredible sixty million tons of cargo per year by 1939 – well over one-third of all British trade, and the reason why east London generally and the docks in particular were to take such a pounding in the next war.

85. K2 Red Telephone Box

Burlington House, Piccadilly, W1

As a significant part of twentieth-century urban infra-structure, the red telephone box is now as redundant as the Routemaster, but like that much-loved icon (in whose image the New Bus For London has reportedly been created) it is still as familiar to visitors to London as Tower Bridge or the traditional black cab.

The first of a long line, Kiosk No. 1 – or the K1 – is curiously something you won't find on the streets of London, as its design was rejected by the authori-ties when it was first introduced in 1920. The concept was good, however, and a need well established, so a competition to design a better box was held under the auspices of the Royal Fine Art Commission. The win-ning design came from the architect Sir Giles Gilbert Scott, a trustee of Sir John Soane's Museum, which is significant since his design was topped by a truncated dome similar in form to the one on Soane's tomb at St Pancras Old Church.

From 1926 onwards the earliest of these K2s were built of wood and intended (as at Burlington House) to be situated under cover. For more exposed locations Scott proposed making them of mild steel, but the General Post Office favoured cast iron while insisting on red paint for extra visibility rather than Scott's muted silver with its greeny-grey interior.

Unfortunately the cast iron boxes were heavy and enormously expensive, and with the K2 reserved for London a much cheaper K6 box was designed for use elsewhere in the country. Both are now regarded quite rightly as classics of British industrial design but the K2, still unique to London, is very much the crème de la crème and as a collector's item commands a price of at least £10,000, or around three or four times that of its lesser cousin.

86. 55 Broadway

Westminster, SW1

London's first steel-framed skyscraper, this imposing art deco masterpiece was completed in 1929 as the head-quarters of the Underground Electric Railways Company of London. As the forerunner of today's Transport for London, its cruciform design, by Charles Holden, was intended to express above ground the scale, scope and technical ingenuity of a largely subterranean network of lines, which by this time criss-crossed the metropolis.

Dwarfed by its contemporaries across the Atlantic (New York's Chrysler Building is around six times higher) a height of 180 feet nevertheless made an extremely bold statement, even if much of it remained unoccupied until the late 1940s as a result of objections lodged by the London Fire Brigade. In the event of a fire, brigade commanders insisted, they lacked ladders of a suitable length to reach the upper storeys of the central tower.

Notwithstanding the very traditional choice of Portland stone for the façades, the transatlantic 'Jazz Age' influence is clear to see in the building's design and marked something of a brave departure in a city where Edwardian and imperial tastes still had a few years left to run. More controversial still was the building's sculptural decoration by Jacob Epstein, one of many Jewish émigré artists swelling the population of London at this time. Not for the first time in London artistic mores were running years ahead of public taste and, following protests, certain portions of Epstein's stonework – two naked figures carved at first-floor level – were quietly trimmed back.

87. 'No News Today'

Savoy Hill, Strand, WC2

On 18 April 1930, at 6.30 p.m. from a studio on Savoy Hill, an announcer for the British Broadcasting Corporation reported, quite seriously, that there was no news to be reported that day. It was Good Friday, and to fill the silence listeners were invited to enjoy some piano playing.

The BBC was at the time relatively young, and decidedly under-resourced compared to the behemoth of today. Occupying the site just off the Strand of John of Gaunt's medieval palace (see chapter 6, York Watergate) its studios were modest too and, until the installation of news agency tape machines, much of the material for news bulletins still came from Reuters news agency and government departments rather than the BBC's own staff.

Today it is inconceivable that such a bland announcement would be considered appropriate, but that it was is a reflection of how London could lie at the heart of a global empire yet be almost entirely insulated from it. In fact, on the very day of the announcement, among other stories worthy of report, a group of Bengali radicals were promoting rebellion against the British Raj by attacking a key armoury and communication lines in the important transport hub of Chittagong.

The uprising failed as the insurgents were eventually surrounded by thousands of troops, and nearly one hundred men were killed in the ensuing gunfight. But in those days news travelled slowly, if at all, and with no one on the spot to report back to London about this important step on the road towards Indian independence the BBC decided to broadcast a little light music – and for many months the public remained none the wiser.

88. Penguin Enclosure, London Zoo

Regent's Park, NW1

It was a New York arts administrator who first described Adolf Hitler as 'my best friend. He shakes the tree and I collect the apples' – but London too was immeasurably enriched, artistically and intellectually, by the influx of Jewish refugees fleeing central Europe in the 1930s.

A long list of the most eminent would have to include publishers George Weidenfeld and André Deutsch, philosopher Karl Popper, economist Eric Hobsbawm, Ken Adam (the designer behind so many iconic James

Bond epics), Clement Freud MP, the architectural historian Nikolaus Pevsner and the studio potter Dame Lucy Rie. There were rogues too, of course, including Peter Rachman and the fraudulent, bullying newspaper proprietor Robert Maxwell, but also plenty of artists and architects who left a more positive mark on the city they came to call home.

Among the latter one of the most remarkable was Berthold Lubetkin, who trained in Moscow, Warsaw and Berlin before moving to London to design its first modernist buildings. His Tecton partnership was instrumental in a number of pioneering civic and housing projects, including High Point I and II in north-west London; but ahead of this he created several innovative and highly influential structures at London Zoo including the 1934 penguin pool, which is now Grade I listed.

It seems a bizarre idea but since its earliest days the zoo had always championed first-rate architecture and continues to do so. In the 1820s and 1830s the resident architect was Sir Decimus Burton who also designed two of the terraces around Regent's Park, Wellington Arch and the Hyde Park Screen. And after Lubetkin came Lord Snowdon who created the famous aviary, and Sir Hugh Casson's pavilion for the elephants and rhinos. Cynics have suggested that modernism succeeded here only because animals, unlike people, couldn't object to its dictates and dogma, but the architects have had the last laugh with developments such as the Barbican, Isokon Flats and Trellick Tower now much sought after.

89. Battersea Power Station

SW8

Another of the country's authentic architectural icons, if in part for all the wrong reasons, this Grade II listed former power station has been derelict for the best part of thirty years but at the time of writing it is – yet again – being tipped for redevelopment.

Like the K2 the design, with its elaborate art deco interior, was one of Giles Gilbert Scott's, and like the aforementioned Hoover Factory the building seemed to herald an exciting new industrial age as well as highlighting the huge physical energy and incredible power demands of a large, modern city.

Forceful but uncompromising, the way that the power station looms so ominously over the river must nevertheless have made it a wholly unwelcome addition to the skyline in the 1930s, particularly when viewed from the opposite, more expensive bank. It is also easy to forget what it was built for, and so to overlook that when operating at capacity – with four chimneys belching away and Britain's largest-ever boilers consuming a million tons of coal annually – it would have been a significant and inexhaustible source of choking, year-round pollution.

But the building made an impact on London in other ways too, of course, which explains the extraordinary affection in which it is held today. With numerous movie appearances – from The Beatles in 1965 to Take That nearly half a century later – the incident of Pink Floyd's famous flying pig, and the protracted saga of the building's will-it-won't-it development, this large and prominent site is one in which these days every Londoner seems to have a personal stake.

90. Coram's Fields

Guilford Street, WC1

In the 1730s a rich seafarer Thomas Coram established the Foundling Hospital in Bloomsbury to improve the lot of London children, and almost exactly two hundred years later – with the hospital's extensive grounds earmarked for development – seven precious acres were rescued and set aside for their continued enjoyment. Unique among London parks in that adults are forbidden to enter unless accompanied by someone aged sixteen or under, it includes play areas, a pond, a café and a petting zoo.

A small museum on the same site commemorates the life of Captain Coram and his unusual bequest – the charity bearing his name is still actively helping children in London – and by the main entrance a stone pillar contains a niche in which eighteenth-century working-class mothers could deposit their babies in the knowledge that they would be collected, cared for and given a better chance at life.

91. Post Office Research Station

Flowers Close, NW2

By the mid-1930s it was becoming clear to the authorities in London (if not yet to the wider public) that another war in Europe was in prospect, and beneath a block of housing association flats in Dollis Hill is evidence that the threat from a resurgent Germany was being taken very seriously indeed.

Dating back to 1925 the building was officially opened a few years later by Prime Minister Ramsay MacDonald, although little about its name or appearance would have aroused much interest at that time. As a research facility it notched up an impressive record, however, with staff employed here developing Colossus, the world's first programmable electronic computer, and later ERNIE, which for years selected the winning Premium Bond numbers, as well as leading the way for numerous advances in telecommunications.

Designed by east London-born engineer Thomas Flowers – now commemorated in the building's address – Colossus was to play a vital role in the war effort as part of the Bletchley Park top secret code-breaking programme.

The building has an even more remarkable secret, however, namely a large, multilevel underground bunker, code-named Paddock, from which the prime minister, the cabinet and chiefs of staff from the army, navy and air force could safely direct the war.

One of several subterranean citadels – there is another even larger one beneath the vast creeper-clad Admiralty building at the entrance to the Mall – it was constructed amidst great secrecy in 1939 to ensure that the administration of the country would continue when and if German bombs began to rain down on London.

In the event it saw very little use, however, as only two meetings of the War Cabinet were held here before Winston Churchill insisted on a return to central London. Hating the place and never happy in the suburbs, Churchill much preferred the original Cabinet War Rooms situated just off Whitehall. These are now an immensely popular visitor attraction, although one wonders how many of those who walk through them realize they form just a tiny part of an even larger, six-acre complex of underground offices beneath Storey's Gate. Protected by a seventeen-foot-thick concrete shield, which can be seen from the road outside, and still not open to the public, like 'Paddock' it provides a tantalizing glimpse of a London that almost no one knows.

Chapter 11

MODERN TIMES

In London the First World War had on the whole scarred people rather than places, but the Second devastated the city, residents growing accustomed to a landscape of bombsites and burned-out buildings as whole areas were laid waste and more than a million homes badly damaged or destroyed.

Hitler believed he could bomb the British into defeat, but was quickly proved wrong both in London and across the country as a whole. Myths have grown up around the so-called Blitz spirit, but many of the worst affected seemed genuinely to take a strange pride in finding themselves on the front line and, sharing some of the hardships faced by the fighting men, the people remained resolute in their belief that 'we can take it'.

The effects were nevertheless horrifying, although the casualty figures were perhaps surprisingly low given the scale of the destruction and the damage to such significant landmarks as the Tower of London, Westminster Abbey and the House of Commons. The aftermath of the bombing also led to many exciting discoveries – including Roman, Saxon and medieval remains found buried beneath the ruins – and provided an unusual opportunity to remake London. Naturally not all the new buildings were good, some were truly awful, but slowly London emerged from the ashes as it had done after the Great Fire nearly three hundred years before.

92. The Barbican

City of London, EC2

One of the most extensive attempts at refashioning the battered capital, the Barbican development was intended not simply to replace buildings that had been lost but to reverse the longstanding flow of residents out of the historic Square Mile. Providing accommodation for more than 6,500, it was conceived as an entirely new sort of self-contained community with its own shops, nearly a dozen acres of water and public open space, car parking, a restaurant, theatre, cinema, two schools and a concert hall.

The site had been so badly devastated by incendiary bombs that it was said to be possible to walk for half a mile without passing a single intact building. But from the start the rebuilding scheme, while crucial to London, was bedevilled by planning problems and delayed by labour disputes. The first outline designs by Chamberlin, Powell & Bon were ready as early as 1954, but it was to be 1960 before anything was signed off and well into the 1980s before the arts centre – always intended to be very much the heart of the development – was completed and opened by Her Majesty the Queen.

The emphatically modernist architecture still appears uncompromising and quite brutal, and clearly of its time. But it was officially Grade II listed within twenty years of its completion, by which time the complex had achieved many of its aims, becoming an important hub for the arts in London as a whole and a significant destination for visitors to the city. Critics point out that the population is by no means as socially mixed as was first intended: location and demand mean that prices for the 999-year leases have become enormous, and the place empties out each Friday evening as the well-heeled residents decamp to second homes in the country. But the architects conceived it as 'a coherent residential community in which people can live both conveniently and with pleasure' and in this they must be adjudged to have succeeded.

93. BT Tower

Cleveland Street, W1

With growing union unrest, a domestic motor industry bent on committing suicide and the sudden abandonment of many significant aerospace projects, Labour's 1960s dreams of a brand new Britain forged in the white heat of a technological revolution proved a non-starter. Within a very few years it became clear that the hoped for new age would never dawn, although London at least gained one stridently modern landmark, which still looks quite spectacular and remains much loved.

Completed in 1965 and rising to an impressive 619 feet, what was originally known as the Post Office Tower was the creation not of one of that era's star architects but of the Ministry of Works' own Eric Bedford. Intended to provide a platform from which to beam millions of high-energy and microwave radio, television and telephone signals out over the perimeter of the London basin – as it still does today – it was designed to be functional and elegant, although in one fascinating regard it proved to be as hollow as the politicians' promises.

What looks like an imaginative, if slender, circular tower

block, and cleverly engineered to bend eight inches from the vertical in high winds, the structure is in reality no more than a concrete column. This is concealed within circles of steel and glass cladding to give the impression of offices but actually offers no accommodation above the eighth floor besides a couple of observation decks and an expensive restaurant. Situated on the thirty-fourth floor, the latter turns slowly to reveal a wonderful panorama of the city down below – a single revolution takes just over twenty minutes – but sadly the restaurant has been off-limits to the public since 1971 when the IRA exploded a bomb in the gents' loos on the floor below.

Striking and technically ingenious, the building might have heralded an age of similarly innovative structures across the West End, but this never happened and for years most of its neighbours were uninspiring sixties blocks or shabby Georgian survivors. Today, looking down from the top, it is clear that the landscape is changing in this regard with a considerable amount of new building, particularly on the huge vacant site of the old Middlesex Hospital. Much of this is exciting if controversial – historic Fitzrovia is jealously guarded – but even now, nearly fifty years on, it is hard to imagine a single building managing to match the impact or appeal of Eric Bedford's great tower.

94. London E4

Sewardstone, Essex

London's oldest surviving postbox was installed in Cornwall Gardens, W8 in 1866, approximately ten years after the first postcodes were introduced to speed the delivery of mail across the London postal district. As the city continued to expand – becoming the County of London in 1880, and Greater London in 1965 – Royal Mail's system of numbering also became larger and more complex, particularly in those areas where the population was more than averagely dense.

Currently based on six individual lettered zones – NW, N, E, W, SW and SE* – the arrangement follows the compass and is on the whole logical, although certain aspects of it can appear to be quite random. SW1 and SW3, for example, both lie north of the river and are adjacent to each other, whereas SW2 is several miles away on the other side of the Thames. The key to this is in the order in which they are numbered, with the figure 1 being

---

* Of the four compass points S was abolished by the novelist Anthony Trollope during his time as Chief Secretary to the Postmaster General, and later reassigned to Sheffield.

used to denote the central 'head district' after which individual neighbourhoods are ordered alphabetically. Chelsea (SW3) therefore comes after Brixton (SW2) but ahead of Clapham (SW4).

There are nevertheless a number of peculiarities, the reasons for which are not always easy to discern. There is, for example, no district numbered E19; Thamesmead is SE28 despite being alphabetically ahead of SE27 (West Norwood); and, most curiously of all, a small village in the parish of Waltham Abbey in Essex – Sewardstone – is officially classified as 'London E4' even though it lies well outside the boundary of Greater London. The other anomaly is E20, which now describes the area occupied by the former Olympic Park but was hitherto applied to Walford, the fictional setting for the BBC soap *EastEnders*.

95. London Docklands Development Corporation

Isle of Dogs, E14

Responsible for facilitating such large-scale developments as Canary Wharf, Surrey Quays, London City Airport and much else besides, this powerful quango was established in 1981 specifically to regenerate more than eight square miles of derelict land stretching away to the east of Tower Bridge.

The vast complex of docks had recovered well from the pummelling that this part of east London received during the Second World War, but it could not keep pace with the switch to containerization and the impact this had on ship design. Specifically, each new generation of vessel was so much larger than the preceding one that they were becoming too large to dock anywhere but coastal ports (those in the new 'Maersk Triple E' family, for example, are almost a quarter of a mile long and as wide as a six-lane motorway).

At a cost of more than eighty thousand jobs the Port of London consequently found itself grinding to a halt towards the end of the 1970s, a sad end to a history stretching all the way back to the first century (and the foundation of Londinium) and a potential disaster for the local population and economy.

Until being wound up in 1997 the LDDC was charged with finding new uses for some of the more promising of the old buildings – following a pattern already established at St Katharine Docks – and for reclaiming and selling off thousands of acres of land for new developments. The latter involved creating an entirely new communications infrastructure, including approximately one hundred miles of new roads and an entirely new, driverless Docklands Light Railway to more effectively connect the rejuvenated areas with the rest of the capital. By far the largest project of its kind ever undertaken in this country, the work was at times contentious but ultimately hugely successful.

Initially and predictably there was considerable resentment from members of the (largely unemployed) local population who felt squeezed out of their own neighbourhoods by developers and a brash new class of yuppies. By the time the quango was wound up sixteen years later, however, tempers had cooled, and literally millions of square metres of new office and commercial space had been created, together with much better employment prospects and as many as twenty-five thousand new homes. The vast majority of this had been achieved using private sector financing, which ran into many billions of pounds.

Inevitably, given the kind of scale on which the LDDC was required to operate, many of the buildings that sprang up are unremarkable and not all are of outstanding quality. Certainly there is nothing to match the best of the old buildings – like glorious Tobacco Dock, for example, which is Grade I listed – but perhaps this matters less than one might suppose.

The truth is that the development of the old docks created an entirely new London, one not hampered by the existing landscape, nor by restrictive vested interests or the need to preserve what was here already. Because of this the likelihood is that the area will continue to evolve in a way that older parts of London were never free to do, which in turn means that most of the new buildings will probably not survive for long. Instead rapidly escalating land prices, advances in technology and continual changes in the commercial landscape will drive change as never before so that the lifespan of most twentieth- and twenty-first-century structures – even the landmark ones – is likely to be far shorter than anything featured in the earlier sections of this book.

96. 'MI6 Building'

Vauxhall Cross, SW8

For much of the twentieth century Britain's secret services were just that, with few in London aware even of where the likes of MI5 and MI6 were based let alone who they were or what they got up to.

In the early days agents were typically housed in small anonymous buildings scattered around St James's, at least two of which are supposed to have been connected by a secret underground tunnel with an abundance of false nameplates above the doors to deter callers.[*] According

---

[*] For a while MI6 hid behind the identity of the 'Minimax Fire Extinguisher Company' but such ruses rarely worked. During the 1930s German Intelligence knew exactly what was going on and posted agents across the street on a more or less permanent basis to keep an eye on any comings and goings.

to thriller writer and former Cold War spook John le
Carré even the head man was housed on an upper floor
'of a crooked little building at the end of a creepy, spi-
dery corridor and then up a small staircase'. No one
outside a very tight circle of Establishment types would
have known even his name at this time, and security was
reportedly so lax in these shadowy warrens that a Soviet
double agent like Kim Philby was able to take suitcases
full of documents home each weekend to pore over with
his Soviet controllers.

There was a decisive shift in 1994, however, when the
Secret Intelligence Service moved into one of the largest
and most conspicuous buildings on the river. Barely two
years prior to this the existence of the service had not
even been publicly acknowledged, but following a commitment from Prime Minister John Major to 'sweep away
some of the cobwebs surrounding its secrecy' MI6 was
generally assumed to have taken over Sir Terry Farrell's
£280 million postmodern ziggurat.

The move was never formally announced, however,
and officially the green and sand-coloured building is still
known only as No. 85 Vauxhall Cross. But Londoners all
know it as the MI6 building – it has featured in a brace of
James Bond movies, and in 2000 was actually damaged by
a Russian-made rocket – although some conspiracy theo-
rists still suspect the whole thing is an elaborate double
bluff. Their theory is that the real business of spying takes

place somewhere entirely different, which is a nice idea but sounds about as likely as the rumour of another, even longer tunnel that is said to link up with MI5 at Thames House on the other side of the river.

97. Neasden Temple

Brentfield Road, NW10

As described earlier there is nothing new about London's status as one of the world's most ethnically diverse and multicultural cities, and nowhere is there a more flamboyant expression of this than the Bochasanwasi Shri Akshar Purushottam Shri Swaminarayan Mandir.

Completed in 1995 it had room for more than 2,500 worshippers (making it by far the largest Hindu temple outside India) and was the first traditional building of its kind anywhere in Europe. Members of the large Hindu diaspora had previously resorted to using converted secular buildings until – entirely new and bespoke – the Neasden Temple established a new template.

Created by Indian craftsmen and volunteer labour here in London, and making no concessions whatever to its suburban setting or the local vernacular, the design called for nearly three thousand tons of Bulgarian limestone and two thousand tons of Italian Carrara marble to be transported to the subcontinent. On arrival each individual block was sized, carved and numbered before being shipped back to London for assembly.

Wholly self-funded the project was five years in the making and is now one of the capital's most joyous and exciting new buildings. As well as being a world-class exemplar of traditional Asian craftsmanship, and a very real adornment to the streets of this part of north-west London, it is an emphatic statement of the sort of community spirit that really struggles to make an impact in a modern city.

98. BedZED

Sandmartin Way, Hackbridge, SM6

The Beddington Zero Energy Development in the London borough of Sutton is the most colourful, imaginative and pioneering attempt yet to explore a more sustainable means of urban living. Though constructed on a relatively small scale – just eighty-two homes and around twenty workspaces, with minimal parking in order to encourage the use of public transport – BedZED suggests several useful advances for city building and provides a mostly persuasive and attractive model for communities, which are futuristic but still welcoming and humane.

Completed in 2002 on a contaminated brownfield site (Roman ceramics were found during the excavations of what had been a sewage works) the development included a mix of houses, flats and maisonettes, each one carefully designed to reduce the environmental impact of an otherwise normal family life. In particular, using a variety of intelligent technologies residents were able radically to reduce their consumption of resources – for heating (typically by 88 per cent), hot water (57 per cent), electricity (25 per cent) and water (50 per cent) – while the construction of each home used natural and recycled material wherever possible. Local contractors were also used in order to minimize transport costs and boost employment.

The buildings also feature exceptionally high levels of insulation, rain and waste water recycling, and a central, shared combined heat-and-power plant fuelled by organic waste. At the same time scores of integrated photovoltaic panels are used to supplement the conventional energy sources, while distinctive rotating metal cowls on the roofs scoop in fresh air and discharge stale. Finally the development, which was funded by the Peabody Trust – meaning that the more than usually spacious homes are rented rather than owned outright – faces due south. This increases the solar gain through large triple-glazed windows, thereby further reducing heating costs.

The development is also a relatively high density one – essential for any new building in London – but the residents all have their own gardens or roof terraces, with the three-and-a-half acre site also including some community sports facilities. As all this suggests, the impressive reductions in consumption have not been easily achieved, but then the likelihood is that they were never going to be. For some years it has been clear that there will be no single silver bullet solution to the environmental problems we face, and if London is to have the low-carbon future we want it will require this kind of thoughtful planning and not the simple flick of a switch.

99. Boris Bike Docking Station

throughout London

Officially the scheme is called Barclays Cycle Hire but from the start the distinctive blue machines have been known as Boris bikes, a reflection not so much of the unpopularity of Britain's banking sector as of the quite extraordinary popularity of the effervescent and highly idiosyncratic individual during whose tenure as Mayor of London the bikes were introduced.

The idea for them almost certainly wasn't Alexander

Boris de Pfeffel Johnson's, but he has become most closely associated with this latest attempt to get London moving more efficiently. In launching what he himself described as a 'gigantic communist experiment' in 2010, Boris also expressed a wish for the bikes to become another globally recognized London icon, thus putting them on a par with the city's black cabs and red buses.

Despite a few early teething problems (and the inevitable if thankfully rare accidents) this might just happen. Dedicated ranks or docking stations have sprung up everywhere – at the time of writing there are nearly six hundred of them – and far from proving to be a short-lived novelty the eight thousand Canadian-built bikes have very quickly become a familiar sight on London's streets.

On one day in 2012 a record 47,105 individual journeys were undertaken on Boris bikes, and with the first half hour of travel free to subscribers an impressive 49 per cent of users freely admit they took up cycling in London purely because the scheme exists.

For overcrowded London all this could potentially be very good news indeed. The congestion charge has failed to make any significant dents in journey times to cross London and, even if there was room beneath the streets for more tunnels (which there isn't), we lack the resources to create a completely new underground network or indeed to significantly improve the one we already have.

Bikes, then, just might be the answer. Unusually – uniquely – the scheme is set to become the first Transport for London system to fund its running costs entirely, and it also holds out the exciting possibility of London developing a critical mass of regular cyclists. When that happens, and it is beginning to, the hope is that drivers of cars, trucks and buses will begin to adapt their driving style to accommodate these new road users, something that will make the streets of London safer, cleaner and actually slightly faster moving.

100. The Counting House

Cornhill, EC3

A popular pub housed in an old Edwardian bank, the Counting House provides a wonderful example of the way in which the City of London continually reinvents itself and – more unusually – of history in the Square Mile finally coming full circle.

For centuries London merchants mingled with clients and rivals in taverns and, later, in fashionable coffee houses, and plenty of business was successfully concluded in these relatively informal surroundings. The insurance market Lloyds of London, for example, famously evolved from a seventeenth-century establishment of that name on Tower Street. It was here that proprietor Edward Lloyd provided a congenial place for ship owners to gather each afternoon, somewhere news could be exchanged and insurance cover negotiated for any goods being carried on board.

Jonathan's Coffee House similarly became a popular haunt of stockbrokers, especially in the 1690s after they had been excluded from the Royal Exchange on the grounds that they were too rough and rowdy a crowd. The arrangement worked well for many decades, but in the summer of 1772 it was decided that things should be put on a more formal footing, that new premises should be sought and 'called The Stock Exchange, which is to be wrote over the door'.

Sharing in the fluctuating fortunes of the Square Mile, both these organizations expanded enormously and these days occupy large modern buildings carefully tailored to the new ways in which international business is conducted. Over time the banks have undergone similar changes, and equally significant upheavals too, of course. However, while the aforementioned institutions started out selling beverages before moving into business, in the Counting House we find an example of a bank that has reversed the process and gone back to dispensing hospitality.

For those working in the City the greatest upheaval in recent years was the process of rapid deregulation in 1986 that we call the Big Bang. With computerization rapidly becoming the norm, and new ways of trading requiring vast open-plan space rather than carefully structured tiers of enclosed offices, traditional bank premises like this one were no longer fit for purpose.

Many were pulled down and the sites redeveloped, but here the building was carefully restored and remodelled as a bar. As such it has come to encapsulate the way that the City continues to move with the times: where once coffee houses morphed into financial institutions now we have a financial institution reborn as a place where traders and others can meet to discuss business over a drink. And how nice too that, in this particular case, the building's foundations were built upon the remains of London's old Roman basilica, which of course is where our story of London began nearly two thousand years ago.

INDEX